Edwin Hamilton Gifford

The incarnation : a study of Philippians II, 5-11

Edwin Hamilton Gifford

The incarnation : a study of Philippians II, 5-11

ISBN/EAN: 9783741157905

Manufactured in Europe, USA, Canada, Australia, Japa

Cover: Foto ©Andreas Hilbeck / pixelio.de

Manufactured and distributed by brebook publishing software (www.brebook.com)

Edwin Hamilton Gifford

The incarnation : a study of Philippians II, 5-11

THE INCARNATION

A STUDY OF
PHILIPPIANS II. 5-11

BY

E. H. GIFFORD, D.D.

FORMERLY ARCHDEACON OF LONDON, AND CANON OF ST. PAUL'S

NEW YORK
DODD, MEAD & CO.
149-151 FIFTH AVENUE
1897

CORRIGENDA

Page 10, footnote, in the Hebrew word, *for* final *Caph*, *read Resh*.
,, 23, line 3, *insert* " after Θεῷ.
,, 32, *for* " Rheims Bible," *read* " Rhemish Testament."
,, 41, footnote, *for* " Gwyn," *read* " Gwynn."
,, 58, line 10, *delete* comma after ἴσα.
,, 75, ,, 17, *insert* "to human slavery" after δοῦλος.
,, 124, ,, 4, *read* In Aristotle's teaching, as Bishop Lightfoot says, "there are two elements or principles or causes of things; the matter, the substratum supporting the qualities, and the form, the aggregate of the qualities. The form he calls indifferently εἶδος or μορφή, etc.
,, 157, ,, 12, *insert* comma after "omniscience."

PREFACE

THE interpretation of Philippians ii. 5-11, which forms the first part of the present little volume, was originally published as two articles in *The Expositor* for September and October 1896.

Several friends, upon whose judgment I could most fully rely, desired to see the substance of the articles re-published, with additions, in a more permanent and convenient form. This I have now been able to accomplish through the kindness of Messrs. Hodder and Stoughton, the publishers of *The Expositor*.

My purpose throughout has been simply

to establish the true interpretation of St. Paul's language, without attempting to discuss the various dogmatic theories which profess to be deduced from it, except in so far as they are based upon representations of the Apostle's meaning, which I can only regard as mistaken and misleading.

In the historical notes, which form the second part of the volume, I have endeavoured to trace briefly the origin and course of certain errors of interpretation which have been long and widely prevalent in foreign Protestant theology, and have recently begun to find favour in our own country.

The tendency in modern thought to give especial prominence to the earthly life and human character of Christ is doubtless, in many cases, the result of a genuine and earnest desire to strengthen men's faith in the great doctrine of the Incarnation. And we cannot but sympathise with the effort to pourtray the "Perfect Man" in all the reality of our human nature, as helping to produce a livelier sense of the sympathy, compassion, and self-sacrificing love of Him who could "be touched with the feeling of our infirmities," and "tempted in all points like as we are, yet without sin."

On the other hand, there is cause to fear lest humanitarian views of our Saviour's life on earth, if regarded too exclusively and pressed too far, may tend, in minds less learned and less devout, to obscure that glory of the Incarnate Word, which was beheld by the Apostles, "a glory as of the only-begotten of the Father."

But however we may regard the tendency of some recent theories of the Incarnation, there can be but one opinion of the danger of speculative theology based upon erroneous interpretation of the language of Holy Scripture. And that is the danger which I humbly and earnestly seek to avert.

My best thanks are due to the Rev. Dr. Taylor, Master of St. John's College, Cambridge, and to the Rev. Dr. Bright, Canon of Christ Church, Oxford, for the valuable suggestions which I have received from them.

E. H. GIFF(

ARLINGTON HOUSE, OXFORD,
March 1897.

CONTENTS

PART I

	PAGE
I. THE CONTEXT . . .	4
II. THE SUBJECT . .	6
III. ὑπάρχων: (a) PRE-EXISTENCE .	8
III. ὑπάρχων: (b) CONTINUED EXISTENCE	11
IV. ἐν μορφῇ θεοῦ . .	22
V. οὐχ ἁρπαγμὸν ἡγήσατο τὸ εἶναι ἴσα θεῷ	36

	PAGE
VI. ἀλλὰ ἑαυτὸν ἐκένωσεν	71
VII. μορφὴν δούλου λαβών	74
VIII. ἐν ὁμοιώματι ἀνθρώπων γενόμενος	83
IX. καὶ σχήματι εὑρεθεὶς ὡς ἄνθρωπος	88
X. ἐταπείνωσεν ἑαυτόν	89
XI. THE EXALTATION	91

PART II

NOTES ON THE HISTORY OF VARIOUS INTERPRETATIONS . 103

PART I

PHILIPPIANS II. 5–11

Τοῦτο φρονεῖτε ἐν ὑμῖν ὃ καὶ ἐν Χριστῷ Ἰησοῦ, ὃς ἐν μορφῇ Θεοῦ ὑπάρχων οὐχ ἁρπαγμὸν ἡγήσατο τὸ εἶναι ἴσα Θεῷ, ἀλλὰ ἑαυτὸν ἐκένωσεν μορφὴν δούλου λαβών, ἐν ὁμοιώματι ἀνθρώπων γενόμενος· καὶ σχήματι εὑρεθεὶς ὡς ἄνθρωπος ἐταπείνωσεν ἑαυτὸν γενόμενος ὑπήκοος μέχρι θανάτου, θανάτου δὲ σταυροῦ· διὸ καὶ ὁ Θεὸς αὐτὸν ὑπερύψωσεν, καὶ ἐχαρίσατο αὐτῷ τὸ ὄνομα τὸ ὑπὲρ πᾶν ὄνομα, ἵνα ἐν τῷ ὀνόματι Ἰησοῦ πᾶν γόνυ κάμψῃ ἐπουρανίων καὶ ἐπιγείων καὶ καταχθονίων, καὶ πᾶσα γλῶσσα ἐξομολογήσηται ὅτι Κύριος Ἰησοῦς Χριστὸς εἰς δόξαν Θεοῦ πατρός.

Have this mind in you which was also in Christ Jesus; who, **subsisting**[1] in the form of God, counted it not a prize **that he was**[2] on an equality with God, but emptied himself by taking the form of a servant, being made in the likeness of men; and being found in fashion as a man, he humbled himself, becoming obedient *even* unto death, yea, the death of the cross. Wherefore God also hath highly exalted him and given him the Name which is above every name: that at the Name of Jesus every knee should bow, of *things* in heaven, and things in earth, and *things* under the earth: and that every tongue should confess that Jesus Christ is Lord, to the glory of God the Father.

[1] R.V. *being.* Marg. Gr. *being originally.*
[2] R.V. *to be.*

THE INCARNATION:

PHILIPPIANS II. 5-11

IF an apology is needed for adding to the numberless attempts to determine the true meaning of St. Paul's words in this celebrated passage, it may be found in the fact that we still meet with the widest diversities of interpretation in the current theology of the day.[1]

---

[1] An interesting example of this wide divergence of opinion between able and learned theologians occurs in a review in *The Guardian*, 1st January 1896, of Canon Gore's *Dissertations on Subjects connected with the Incarnation*, Murray, 1895: "The next step in the argument is the discussion of the famous passage in St. Paul (*Phil.* ii. 5-11). Here Mr. Gore takes 'form' in both cases in its strict technical sense, and in this we cannot but think that he falls into an error, which, if it be an

There is, however, one point on which all are agreed, namely, that the passage is of primary importance in relation to the fundamental doctrine of the Christian religion, the Incarnation of the Son of God.

But even among those who profess to

error, is one of a highly misleading kind. 'Form of God' in the sense of 'essence or specific character of God' is a phrase that no Greek philosopher, except perhaps the materialists, ever permitted himself to employ, and, as servitude is a mere relation, 'essence of a slave' is a phrase of no meaning. St. Paul must have been using the word 'form' in a loose, popular sense, as we use the word 'nature.' 'Form of a slave' is defined here by the words 'likeness' and 'fashion,' which immediately follow, as the 'emptying' is defined by 'obedience unto death.'

"There is room, no doubt, for much variety of opinion, but the correct exegesis is the strictest, and in any case the wise interpreter will be very shy of erecting a 'Kenosis doctrine' on a phrase the exact limits of which no man can fix with precise accuracy."

base their interpretations upon a strict examination of the Apostle's language, there seems to be as yet no general agreement, either as to the meaning of the most important words, or as to the grammatical construction and logical connexion of the passage. There is, in fact, little improvement in these respects since the author of an elaborate and important treatise on the subject declared that "the diversity of opinion prevailing among interpreters in regard to the meaning of the principal passage bearing on the subject of Christ's humiliation—that, namely, in the second chapter of St. Paul's Epistle to the Philippians—is enough to fill the student with despair, and to afflict him with intellectual paralysis."[1]

[1] The Rev. Prof. A. B. Bruce, D.D., *The Humiliation of Christ*, p. 11.

1. *The Context*

In approaching the interpretation of a passage so full of acknowleged difficulties, it is desirable first to notice briefly its connexion with the preceding context. There the Apostle's purpose is happily too clear to be obscured by any diversity of interpretation. St. Paul has been encouraging his beloved converts at Philippi to "stand fast in one spirit, with one soul, striving for the faith of the Gospel." He entreats them to make his joy in them complete by adding to their faith and courage the crowning graces of humility and self-denying love. He pleads with them by every motive of Christian fellowship, and not least by their personal affection for himself, and their sympathy with his sufferings in behalf of Christ, to "be of the same mind, having the same love, being of one accord, of one mind." "Let nothing," he says, "be done through strife or vainglory; but in lowliness of mind let each esteem other better than himself. Look not every man on his own things, but every man also on the things of others. Let this mind be in you, which was also in Christ Jesus."

These earnest and loving entreaties the Apostle proceeds to enforce, by setting forth our Blessed Lord Himself as the supreme example of humility, self-sacrifice, and love; and he is thus led on to speak of those deepest and holiest mysteries of the Christian Faith, the Incarnation of the Son of God, His voluntary self-abasement, His obedience "even unto death, yea, the death of the Cross." In order that this view of the general connexion of the passage may help to guide us to a right interpretation, the point which must especially be borne in mind is, that the Incarnation and human life of our Lord are set before us as the perfect example of the principle enjoined in v. 4, "Not looking each to his own things, but each also to the things of others."

II. *The Subject*

In passing to the direct interpretation of our passage, we have to notice, first, that there has been much discussion whether Christ, as denoted by the relative pronoun ὅς, is regarded only in His life on earth, or also as the Eternal Word, which "was in the beginning with God, and was God."

In answer to this question we might too easily be tempted to argue, as Meyer does, that ὅς denotes "the subject of what follows; consequently Christ Jesus, but in *the prehuman state*, in which He the Son of God

... was with God"; the *human* state being first introduced by the words in v. 7, "He emptied Himself."

In arguing thus we should assume by anticipation a meaning in what follows, which is much contested, and remains as yet to be proved. For we are reminded by Meyer himself that it is still a point of Lutheran orthodoxy "to regard the *incarnate historical* Christ, the Λόγος ἔνσαρκος, as the subject meant by ὅς."[1] It is therefore safer and more strictly correct to say with Hofmann, in his Commentary on the Epistle, that "the Apostle, speaking of Him who was known to His readers under the name of Christ Jesus, asserts something which He did when in a state of existence described as *being in the form of God.*"

[1] *Commentary on Philippians*, p. 79. Eng. Trans.

III. ὑπάρχων: (a) *Pre-existence*

(a) The meaning given to ὑπάρχων in the margin of the Revised Version (Gr. *being originally*) is so generally recognised among scholars, that we need not dwell upon it, except to point out that this sense is strongly marked in several passages of St. Paul's epistles.

1 Cor. xi. 7, "*For a man indeed ought not to have his head veiled, forasmuch as he is* (ὑπάρχων) *the image and glory of God.*"

Here the word evidently points to what man is by his original creation in the image of God.

2 Cor. viii. 17, "*For indeed he accepted our exhortation; but being himself* (ὑπάρχων) *very earnest, he went forth unto you of his own accord.*"

Here "himself" is not expressed by a

separate word in the Greek, nor does it appear in the Authorised Version, but has been rightly added by the Revisers, to bring out the meaning of ὑπάρχων.

On Galatians ii. 14, "*If thou being a Jew livest as do the Gentiles*," Bishop Lightfoot remarks that Ἰουδαῖος ὑπάρχων is "very emphatic," "born and bred a Jew." So Meyer, "although a born Jew"; and Howson (*Speaker's Commentary*): "The Greek means more than this ('*being*'), and denotes that he was 'a Jew by birth,' a Jew *to begin with*."

This well-established meaning of ὑπάρχων at once excludes the many attempts which have been made to limit the description, *being in the form of God*, to the time of Christ's sojourn upon earth.

In this latter sense it has been thought, for instance, to refer to the divine majesty and power which Jesus manifested during His ministry, either in His miracles, or generally in His words and works, as when St. John says (i. 14) "*We beheld His glory, the glory as of the only begotten of the Father.*"

Others have referred "*the form of God*" to some *special* manifestation of divine glory, such as occurred at His Baptism[1] and Transfiguration.

---

[1] Dr. Resch, *Texte u. Untersuchungen*, Band v. Heft 4, AGRAPHA, pp. 367 ff., argues from the language of the ancient Syriac Baptismal Office of Severus that "*the form of God*" refers to the glorification of Christ in the waters of Jordan. He supposes that in the "Ur-Evangelium" some Hebrew word, perhaps תֹאַר," occurred in the narrative of the glorification, and was translated μορφή by St. Paul. "In accordance with the heavenly voice, *This is My beloved Son*, Paul thus describes the condition of Jesus, in the glorification at the Jordan by the words in Phil. ii. 6ᵃ ὃς

Against all such interpretations it is sufficient to reply, that the meaning of ὑπάρχων, in its connexion with the following context, clearly implies a state existing prior to the point of time at which our Lord *took upon Him the form of a servant, and was made in the likeness of men.*

III. ὑπάρχων: (*b*) *Continued Existence*

This brings us to a second question, which, though not less essential to the right interpretion of ὑπάρχων ἐν μορφῇ Θεοῦ in its relation to the context, has been either altogether overlooked or misunderstood even by the best scholars and interpreters. Thus according to Meyer the clause "simply

ἐν μορφῇ Θεοῦ ὑπάρχων, and in Phil. ii. 6[b] as εἶναι ἴσα Θεῷ.

narrates the former divinely glorious position, which he afterwards gave up."

Even Bishop Lightfoot, to whom every student of this epistle is so deeply indebted, and who is usually so extremely accurate, writes as follows:[1] "Before attempting to discover what is implied by μορφῇ Θεοῦ, it will be necessary to clear the way by disposing of a preliminary question. Does the expression ἐν μορφῇ Θεοῦ ὑπάρχων refer to the pre-incarnate or the incarnate Christ?"

This statement of the question is evidently incomplete, and in fact misleading. It assumes that the clause must refer *exclusively* either to Christ's pre-existent state or to His incarnate state; it thus excludes the obvious and most important alternative, that it *may apply to both*.

[1] *Philippians*, Ed. 1891, p. 131.

In the present tendency of theological speculation in England concerning *the fulness of the Godhead* in the Incarnate Christ, and the opposite doctrine of *Kenoticism*, it is much to be regretted that the third alternative was not taken into consideration by so eminent an interpreter of St. Paul as the late Bishop of Durham. The omission appears to have arisen from an idea that ὑπάρχων must "be referred to *a point of time* prior to the Incarnation."

This expression "*point of time*" (the italics are mine) occurs three times on pp. 131, 132; and its use prejudges the interpretation of the whole passage by implying, unconsciously perhaps on the Bishop's part, that "*the form of God*" did not continue during the ministry on earth.

The true force of the participle ὑπάρχων

is well expressed by Dean Gwynn in his admirable interpretation of the epistle in the *Speaker's Commentary*: "Its tense (Imperfect) contrasted with the following Aorists points to indefinite *continuance* of being."[1]

I hope to show that this meaning is fully confirmed (1) by the nature of the Imperfect tense, (2) by the use of ὑπάρχων in the New Testament and especially in the writings of St. Paul, and (3) by the testimony of very early Christian writers.

(1) Jelf, *Greek Grammar*, § 395: "The Imperfect is to time past what the Present is to time present; both express an action yet in course of performance, and not yet completed"; or, we may add, a

[1] Estius perceived the true force of ὑπάρχων, *qui cum esset ac sit*, though he called it less correctly a *Present* participle.

state in course of continuance not yet ended.

Green, *Grammar of New Testament Dialect*, p. 10: "The essential time signified by the PRESENT and IMPERFECT Tenses is that of a continued or habitually repeated action." Compare p. 100: "The Participle conveys 'the idea of essential time belonging to the particular tense from which the participle is derived.'"

(2) (*a'*) This general property of the imperfect participle may be illustrated first by the use of ὤν in the New Testament in combination with an Aorist. John xi. 49 ἀρχιερεὺς ὢν τοῦ ἐνιαυτοῦ ἐκείνου εἶπεν αὐτοῖς. John xxi. 19 τοσούτων ὄντων οὐκ ἐσχίσθη τὸ δίκτυον.

Would it be reasonable to say that the *states* indicated by the participles ὤν and ὄντων ceased when the action described by the finite verbs occurred?

For other examples see Winer, *Grammar of N.T. Greek*, § xlv. 1, (2), *b*.

(β') But it will be more satisfactory to observe the use of ὑπάρχων itself. Luke xxiii. 50 Ἰωσὴφ βουλευτὴς ὑπάρχων ... οὗτος προσελθὼν τῷ Πειλάτῳ ᾐτήσατο τὸ σῶμα. Acts ii. 30 προφήτης οὖν ὑπάρχων ... προϊδὼν ἐλάλησεν.

Are we to suppose that Joseph of Arimathea ceased to be a "counsellor" as soon as he *begged the body of Jesus*, or David a prophet when he *spake of the resurrection of Christ*?

(γ') The most complete proof of all is St. Paul's own use of ὑπάρχων. 2 Cor. viii. 17 σπουδαιότερος δὲ ὑπάρχων αὐθαίρετος ἐξῆλθεν πρὸς ὑμᾶς... xii. 16 ἀλλ' ὑπάρχων πανοῦργος δόλῳ ὑμᾶς ἔλαβον.

Did Titus cease to be zealous at the moment of starting to visit the Corinthians?

Or does St. Paul mean, in his ironical statement, that, in the opinion of the Corinthians, he ceased to be crafty as soon as he had once caught them with guile? It is impossible, I think, to find or imagine passages more exactly parallel in grammatical construction to Philippians ii. 6 than these two examples of St. Paul's own use of ὑπάρχων.

Another strictly parallel passage is Romans iv. 19 κατενόησε τὸ ἑαυτοῦ σῶμα [ἤδη] νενεκρωμένον, ἑκατονταέτης που ὑπάρχων.

In this case it would be manifestly absurd to say that the state indicated by ὑπάρχων ("*being about a hundred years old*") ceased when Abraham "*considered his own body as good as dead.*"

The only other instances of ὑπάρχων in

St. Paul's writings are 1 Corinthians xi. 7; Galatians i. 14, ii. 14, which are not so exactly parallel to Philippians ii. 6, because in them ὑπάρχων is not combined with an Aorist: but in neither of them is there anything to indicate an immediate cessation of the state described by the participial clause.

So far then as the principles of grammatical construction and the writer's usage are concerned, it is unreasonable to assume that Christ ceased to be "*in the form of God*," when he "*emptied Himself, and took upon Him the form of a servant.*"

(3) The true meaning of ὑπάρχων is clearly seen in a very early, seemingly the earliest, direct quotation of Philippians ii. 6, in the celebrated letter of the Churches of Lyons and Vienne to their Christian brethren in Asia (Euseb. *Hist. Eccl.* v. c. 2).

Those who had suffered torture in the persecution are thus described:

"They were so zealous in their imitation of Christ, *who being in the form of God counted it not a prize to be on an equality with God,*—that though they were (ὑπάρχοντες) in such honour, and had borne witness not once nor twice, but many times,—having been brought back to prison from the wild beasts covered with burns and scars and wounds,—yet they neither proclaimed themselves martyrs, nor suffered us to address them by that name."

These men are held up as zealous imitators of Christ's humility in refusing the title which really belonged to them. Had they ceased to be held in honour as martyrs, there could have been no humility in not proclaiming or accepting the title. Only as having been and still being (ὑπάρχοντες) in honour could they be said to imitate Christ's humility.

That ὑπάρχων was considered by the Greek Fathers to include this idea of continuance, is clear from their constant interpretation of the passage as proving that Christ was at once both God and Man.

It is enough for the present to quote a passage from S. Chrysostom's Commentary on the Epistle, *Hom.* vi. § 3, by which the full meaning of the word is well illustrated: Διὰ τί μὴ εἶπεν, ἐν μορφῇ Θεοῦ γενόμενος, ἀλλ', Ὑπάρχων; Ἴσον ἐστὶ τοῦτο τῷ εἰπεῖν, Ἐγώ εἰμι Ὁ Ὤν.

The force of ὑπάρχων is extremely well expressed by Bengel: "In that *form of God* the Son of God *was existing* from eternity: nor did He cease to exist therein when He came in the flesh, but rather, so far as it concerns His human nature, began to exist therein. And since He was in that form, which is His own excellence as Lord, it was free to Him, even according to His human nature as soon as He assumed it, to be on an equality with God (*pariter Deo*), to adopt such a manner of life and appearance (*victu cultuque uti*) as would correspond to His dignity, so that He might be received and treated by all creatures as their Lord: but He did otherwise."

From the omission to notice this meaning of continued existence in St. Paul's use of ὑπάρχων it has been wrongly assumed that the existence *in the form of God* must have ceased at the moment indicated by the verb ἐκένωσεν, and this assumption is one of several causes tending to the erroneous view that what Christ laid aside was the μορφὴ Θεοῦ.

IV. ἐν μορφῇ Θεοῦ.

Of the phrase "*form of God*" there are two distinct and opposite interpretations, even among those who agree with what has been shown above, that it describes something which Christ already possessed before His Incarnation.

By some "*the form of God*" is limited, as by Meyer, to "the divine appearance" of which Christ by His Incarnation "divested Himself,"[1] "the former divinely glorious position which He afterwards gave up,"[2] "the glory visible at the throne of God."[3]

In this sense it is said to be "not essentially different" from τὸ εἶναι ἴσα Θεῷ. This latter "must in substance denote the same thing, namely, the divine *habitus* of

[1] Commentary, p. 78. [2] p. 79. [3] p. 80.

Christ, which is expressed, as to its *form of appearance*, by ἐν μορφῇ Θεοῦ ὑπάρχων, and, as to its internal *nature*, by τὸ εἶναι ἴσα Θεῷ.[1]"

In this interpretation, which will be fully discussed below, the "form" or condition expressed by μορφὴ Θεοῦ, however glorious and majestic, is regarded as separable, and, at the Incarnation, actually separated from the essential and unchangeable nature of God.

I have referred to Meyer, because he appears to be the ablest supporter of this sense of μορφὴ Θεοῦ. He is followed by many modern commentators. Thus Alford[2] speaks of "the act of laying aside the form of God," and says again, "He emptied himself of the μορφὴ Θεοῦ."

According to Wiesinger, "μορφή is equivalent neither to οὐσία or φύσις, nor to *status* or *conditio*, but to *form, figure, outline;* in

[1] p. 81 *fin.*   [2] Note on v. 8.

general it denotes the external appearance and representation, consequently just the very opposite of οὐσία, in so far as this denotes what lies beneath the form, and comes to be represented in it. The signification οὐσία is besides rejected by the context; as, at v. 7 with reference to the μορφὴ Θεοῦ it is said ἐκένωσεν ἑαυτόν, which certainly cannot be the case in reference to His divine nature."

Hofmann (*Philippians*, 1875, p. 61),[1] says that "the conceptions μορφὴ Θεοῦ and μορφὴ δούλου mutually exclude one another."

Dr. Bruce (*Humiliation of Christ*, p. 28) writes: "This act of self-exinanition involved ... an exchange, absolute or relative, of the form of God for the form of a servant."

Last, not least, Thomasius (*Christi Person u. Werk*, ii. 415) writes: "He emptied

[1] Note on v. 7.

Himself of the μορφὴ Θεοῦ, as is shown by the antithesis μορφὴ δούλου.

"That μορφή is neither directly οὐσία, nor φύσις, nor *status*, but indicates the *forma*, the appearance (*Erscheinung*) in which any one presents himself, we may regard as the general result of the recent exposition of our passage."

In all such interpretations it is assumed:

(1) That the μορφὴ Θεοῦ is something separable from the οὐσία or φύσις, the *essence* or *nature* of God;

(2) That the μορφὴ Θεοῦ is either (*a*) equivalent to τὸ εἶναι ἴσα Θεῷ, (*b*) or that the latter phrase expresses "the internal *nature*," and the μορφή "*the form of appearance*" of Christ's deity.

I shall endeavour to show that each of these assumptions is erroneous.

(1) That μορφή is inseparable from οὐσία and φύσις, which can have no actual existence (ἐνεργείᾳ) without μορφή, but only a potential existence (δυνάμει).

(2) That μορφὴ Θεοῦ and τὸ εἶναι ἴσα Θεῷ are (a) not equivalent, but in (b) their proper meanings are directly reversed.

If we can succeed in establishing these points, I believe that we shall have removed the chief sources of the extraordinary confusion and uncertainty by which the interpretation of the passage has been obscured.

(1) μορφή. The late Bishop Lightfoot, in his admirable essay (*Philippians*, p. 127), has examined the use of the words μορφή and σχῆμα with a completeness which leaves little or nothing to be desired.

He has shown that while σχῆμα "denotes the figure, shape, fashion of a thing," and "altogether suggests the idea of something changeable, fleeting, unsubstantial," on the other hand, μορφή, even in its original meaning as applied to things visible, denotes the one *form* which is proper to the thing as such, and cannot change so long as the nature is the same. "The μορφή of a definite thing, as such, for instance, of a lion or a tree, is one only, while its σχῆμα may change every minute."

In passing to the higher philosophic sense of μορφή, Bishop Lightfoot quotes the passages of Plato, *Phaedo*, pp. 103 E, 104 A, as showing that "in Plato's language the μορφή is the impress of the 'idea' on the individual, or, in other words, the specific character."

Of these two passages the latter is the simpler and more decisive: "Not only is the same name always claimed for the εἶδος itself, but also for something else which is not the εἶδος, and yet has its μορφή always whenever it exists." Plato's meaning is well illustrated by a remark of Sir Alexander Grant: "The Platonic idea was meant to be not only an ἰδέα, or absolute existence transcending the world of space and time, but also an εἶδος, or universal nature manifesting itself in different individuals."[1]

But it is in Aristotle that the use of μορφή becomes frequent, and its philosophical meaning most clearly defined. As Dr. Lightfoot writes: "There are, according to his teaching, two elements, or principles, or causes of things; the matter, the substratum supporting the qualities, and the form, the aggregate of the qualities. The form he calls indifferently εἶδος or μορφή." The last sentence requires some modification: for

[1] Sir A. Grant, *Aristot. Nic. Eth.* I. vi. 10.

while in most passages no distinction seems to be made between the two words, they are elsewhere very clearly distinguished. Of the first sort is the passage *De Anima*, II. i. 1 Λέγομεν δὴ γένος ἕν τι τῶν ὄντων τὴν οὐσίαν, ταύτης δὲ τὸ μὲν ὡς ὕλην, ὃ καθ' αὑτὸ μὲν οὐκ ἔστι τόδε τι, ἕτερον δὲ μορφὴν καὶ εἶδος, καθ' ἣν ἤδη λέγεται τόδε, καὶ τρίτον τὸ ἐκ τούτων. Here εἶδος and μορφή are used indifferently for the specific character which must be added to the matter to give actual existence to any individual thing.

On the other hand, a clear distinction is drawn in Aristot. *de Coelo*, I. ix. 1 ἕτερόν ἐστιν αὐτὴ καθ' αὑτὴν ἡ μορφὴ καὶ μεμιγμένη μετὰ τῆς ὕλης. Here we see that while μορφή may be regarded *per se* in the same abstract sense as εἶδος, *i.e.* as the *specific character*, it also denotes the concrete realisation, what is called by Plotinus (463 B) τὸ ἐν ὕλῃ εἶδος, the τόδε τι, or existing individual thing.

μορφή is therefore properly the nature or essence, not in the abstract, but as actually subsisting in the individual, and retained as long as the individual itself exists.

Thus in the passage before us μορφὴ Θεοῦ is the Divine nature actually and inseparably subsisting in the Person of Christ.

It is important to remember that this sense of μορφή was familiar to the contemporaries of St. Paul, as is proved by the passages quoted by Bishop Lightfoot from Plutarch and Philo Judaeus.

The former, in describing Plato's doctrine of the genesis of the soul (*Moral.* p. 1013 C) writes thus: " For this world itself and each of its parts consists of a corporeal and a metaphysical (νοητῆς) essence, of which the one supplied the matter and substratum, and the other the form and specific character (μορφὴν καὶ εἶδος) to the thing produced."

Again, in p. 1022 E, where some preceding words have been lost, there remain the following: κατὰ τὰ αὐτὰ ἔχων ὡς μορφὴ καὶ εἶδος.

Philo Judaeus (*de Vict. Off.*, otherwise *de Sacrificantibus*, § 13, p. 261 M): "That which has been mutilated is robbed of its quality and specific character (τὴν ποιότητα καὶ τὸ εἶδος), and is nothing else, properly speaking, than formless matter (ἄμορφος ὕλη)." . . . "But he made use of the incorporeal powers, which are properly called ideas, in order that every genus should receive its proper form (μορφήν)."

In the history of our English Bible we find reason to believe that the translators of A.D. 1611 consciously used the word "form" in this philosophical sense. Thus Wyclif wrote: "in the fourme of God," and "taking the fourme of a servaunt."

This was altered much for the worse by Tyndale (A.D. 1534) into "the shape of God," and the shape of a servaunte," and so it remained in Cranmer's Bible (A.D. 1539), and the Geneva (A.D. 1557). But in the Rheims Bible (A.D. 1582) the word "forme" was restored in both places, and this was adopted in the Authorised Version (A.D. 1611).

It may possibly be asked what reason we have to think that the translators of A.D. 1611 were familar with the philosophical sense of the word "*form.*" On this point we have excellent testimony.

The first edition of Hooker's *Ecclesiastical Polity* was published in 1594. In Book I. c. iii. § 4 he speaks of "those forms which give them (things natural) their being";

and he adds in a note: "Form in other creatures is a thing proportionable unto the soul in living creatures. Sensible it is not, nor otherwise discernible than only by effects. According to the diversity of inward forms, things of the world are distinguished unto their kinds."

In 1620 Bacon's *Novum Organon* was published, and in Book II. Aphorism iv. he gives a definition of "form" remarkably pertinent to our present inquiry. "The form of a nature is such, that given the form the nature infallibly follows. Therefore it is always present, when the nature is present, and universally implies it, and is constantly inherent in it. Again the form is such, that if it be taken away the nature infallibly vanishes. Therefore it is always absent when the nature is absent, and implies its absence, and inheres in nothing else." Again in Aphorism xiii. he says: "The form of a thing is the very thing itself" (Cum enim forma rei sit ipsissima res). On Bacon's use of the word "form" see the preface to the *Philosophical Works* by R. Leslie Ellis, p. 31.

In Aphorism ii., speaking of the word *forms*, he says, "a name which I the rather adopt because it has grown into use and become familiar."

Thus it is clear that the philosophical sense of "form" was as familiar to our translators as that of μορφή to contemporaries of St. Paul.

If this is the true meaning of μορφή when used in its philosophical sense, to say that μορφή is separable from φύσις and οὐσία, and that "they can exist without it," is as manifest an error as to say that the abstract can exist without any concrete, the universal without any individual, goodness without any good thing, the "nature" or "essence" of God without any God.

For the interpretation of "*the form of God*" it is sufficient to say that (1) it includes the whole nature and essence of Deity, and is inseparable from them, since they could have no actual existence without it ; and (2) that it does not include in itself anything "accidental" or separable, such as particular modes of manifestation, or conditions of glory and majesty, which may at one time be attached to the "form," at another separated from it. (3) The Son of God could not possibly divest Himself of "the form of God" at His Incarnation without thereby ceasing to be God: so that in all interpretations which assume that "the form of God" was laid aside when "the form of a servant" was assumed, it is, in fact, however unintentionally and unconsciously, denied that Jesus Christ during His life on earth was really and truly God.

Thus far then we have considered the relation of the passage to the preceding context, the description of the Subject, *"Christ Jesus,"* as pre-existing and continually subsisting (ὑπάρχων) *in the form of God* (ἐν μορφῇ Θεοῦ), and have maintained the primitive interpretation of the latter words as denoting *the fulness of the Godhead*, against various attempts to assign to them some lower meaning.

We now proceed to examine the next clause, the difficulties of which have given occasion to endless discussion and the widest diversities of opinion.

v. οὐχ ἁρπαγμὸν ἡγήσατο τὸ εἶναι ἴσα Θεῷ

In the interpretation of this clause we have to determine the following questions :—

(*a*) What is the meaning of the words τὸ εἶναι ἴσα Θεῷ and their relation to μορφὴ Θεοῦ?

(*b*) Do they denote Christ's condition before His Incarnation, or that to which He was to attain only as His reward?

(*c*) What is the meaning of οὐχ ἁρπαγμὸν ἡγήσατο?

(*a*) In the Revised Version the words ἴσα Θεῷ are translated *on an equality with God*, instead of *equal with God*, as in the Authorised Version.

The change is of great importance to the right interpretation of the whole passage.

The rendering "*equal with God,*" denoting the same essential equality of nature which is already expressed by "*being in the form of God,*" is evidently derived from the Latin Version, "*esse se aequalem Deo,*" which passed at an early period into the theological writings of the Western Church.

It was apparently due at first to the fact that the Latin language had no adequate mode of representing the exact form and meaning of the Greek εἶναι ἴσα Θεῷ.

The neuter plural ἴσα, whether used adverbially or as an adjective, cannot refer to the *one* unchanging nature or essence of Deity, but denotes the various modes or states in which it was possible for that nature to exist and manifest itself as divine.

Unfortunately this force of the neuter plural has not been very generally observed, or not quite accurately expressed.

The general acceptance of the Latin version, *esse se aequalem Deo*, led even such great theologians as Bishop Pearson and Bishop Bull to interpret τὸ εἶναι ἴσα Θεῷ as denoting the equality of *nature*, and therefore as equivalent to ἐν μορφῇ Θεοῦ ὑπάρχων.

Thus Bishop Bull[1] writes: "qui cum in forma Dei (h.e. Deus) esset, adeoque Deo Patri respectu naturae suae aequalis, eam tamen cum Deo aequalitatem sibi non assumpsit, non ut Deum sese gessit, non id palam patefecit," again, "in forma Dei substitisse, Deoque aequalis fuisse ostenditur,"[2] and again, "in forma Dei, adeoque Deo aequalem extitisse." But elsewhere more correctly he writes: "Quod, cum in forma Dei esset, non ostentaverit suam cum Deo ἰσοτιμίαν (id enim significant verba οὐχ ἁρπαγμὸν ἡγήσατο τὸ εἶναι ἴσα Θεῷ)."[3]

Bishop Pearson, referring to Homer, *Od.* xv. 159—

---

[1] *De Jesu Christi Divinitate*, § 19 (vol. vi. p. 347).
[2] *l.c.* ii. c. 3, § 15. See also ii. c. 10, § 3.
[3] *Def. Fid. Nic.* ii. c. 3, § 4.

τὸν νῦν ἶσα θεῷ Ἰθακήσιοι εἰσορόωσιν,

says that "ἶσα has not the nature of an adverb, as belonging to εἰσορόωσιν, but of a noun referred to the antecedent τόν, or including an adverb added to a noun, τὸν νῦν ὡς ἰσόθεον."

But Bishop Pearson was perhaps not altogether unconscious of the weakness of his argument; for he goes on to examine the use of ἶσα in the Septuagint, especially in the book of Job, where it is very frequent, and acknowledges that it is always used there adverbially, but adds, in support of his own view, that it "has not the addition of τὸ εἶναι, in which the strength of his interpretation lies."

We shall presently see that ἶσα, though connected with εἶναι, is still an adverb, not a noun.

Meyer, in accordance with most commentators,[1] rightly observes, that "ἴσα is *adverbial: in like manner*"; but then adds, "This adverbial use has arisen from the frequent employment, even so early as Homer (*Il.* v. 71, xv. 439; *Od.* xi. 304, xv. 519 *al.*), of ἴσα as the case of the object or predicate."

In the passages thus referred to it will at once be seen that ἴσα is simply adverbial.

Il. v. 70   (ὃν) ἔτρεφε δῖα Θεανὼ
              ἴσα φίλοισι τέκεσσι.
xv. 439 (ὃν) ἴσα φίλοισι τοκεῦσιν ἐτίομεν.
Od. xi. 304 τιμὴν δὲ λελόγχασ' ἴσα θεοῖσιν.
xv. 520:
      τὸν νῦν ἴσα θεῷ Ἰθακήσιοι εἰσορόωσιν.

Meyer proceeds: "But as εἶναι, as the abstract substantive verb, does not suit the *adverbial* ἴσα, *pari ratione*, therefore τὸ

[1] Ellicott, Gwyn, Thomasius, etc. Cf. Winer, *Gr.* § xxvii. 3. Meyer, p. 87.

εἶναι must be taken in the sense of *existere;* so that τὸ εἶναι ἴσα Θεῷ does not mean *the being equal to God* (which would be τὸ εἶναι ἴσον Θεῷ), but *the God-equal existence*, existence in the way of parity with God."

Meyer's view of the construction involves two distinct grammatical errors.

First, the assumption that "the abstract substantive verb does not suit the adverbial ἴσα" is contrary both to the opinion of grammarians and to actual usage. For the general principle, that adverbs may stand in the predicate after a verb substantive, see Matthiae, *Gk. Gr.* § 309, C; Bernhardy, *Griech. Syntax*, p. 337; Jelf, *Gk. Gr.* § 374 E, and 375, 3. To the examples commonly quoted, as Eur. *Hec.* 536 σῖγα πᾶς ἔστω λεώς, and Hom. *Il.* ix. 550 Κουρήτεσσι κακῶς ἦν, we may add, as more

"ON AN EQUALITY WITH GOD" 43

closely parallel to the present passage, Thuc. i. 25 χρημάτων δυνάμει ὄντες κατ' ἐκεῖνον τὸν χρόνον ὁμοῖα τοῖς Ἑλλήνων πλουσιωτάτοις, and iii. 14 ἐν οὗ τῷ ἱερῷ ἴσα καὶ ἱκέται ἐσμέν.

Still more decisive, as referring expressly to our present passage, are two examples of the same construction in the Epistle of the Synod of Ancyra, A.D. 358, contained in the account of the Semi-Arians by Epiphanius, *Haer.* 73 § 9 C οὕτω καὶ ὁ υἱὸς ὢν τοῦ Θεοῦ καὶ ἐν μορφῇ ὑπάρχων Θεοῦ, καὶ ἴσα ὢν Θεῷ, κτλ., and § 9 D οὔτε μορφή ἐστι τοῦ Θεοῦ ἀλλὰ Θεοῦ, οὔτε ἴσα ἐστὶ τῷ Θεῷ ἀλλὰ Θεῷ.

These examples fully justify the assertion that εἶναι must be taken as the substantive verb in its usual sense, referred to ὅς as its subject, and followed by ἴσα Θεῷ as an adverbial predicate, as if St. Paul had written more fully τὸ αὐτὸς εἶναι ἶσα Θεῷ, the subject of εἶναι being thus expressed by a pronoun, as in the Latin *esse se*.

Thus it is not the nature or essence, already denoted by μορφή, but the *mode of existence* that is described in this second clause; and one mode of existence may be exchanged for another, though the essential nature is immutable. Let us take St. Paul's own illustration, 2 Cor. viii. 9, "Though He was rich, yet for your sakes He became poor, that ye through His poverty might become rich." Here in each case there is a change of the *mode of existence*, but not of the nature. When a poor man becomes rich, his *mode of existence* is changed, but not his nature as man. It is so with the Son of God; from the rich and glorious *mode of existence* which was the fit and adequate manifestation of His divine nature, He for our sakes descended, in respect of His human life, to the infinitely lower and poorer *mode of existence* which He assumed together with the nature of man.

Secondly, the assertion that "τὸ εἶναι ἴσα Θεῷ does not mean *the being equal to God* (which would be τὸ εἶναι ἴσον Θεῷ), but *the God-equal existence*,"[1] is quite inadmissible.

We may just notice by the way that ἴσον, the accusative, should be ἴσος, referring to the subject of the principal verb ἡγήσατο. But the more serious error lies in making ἴσα Θεῷ an attributive to τὸ εἶναι. That this is Meyer's meaning, is clear from the note in the English translation, "The German is: nicht *das Gotte gleich sein*, sondern, *das gottgleiche Sein*, das Sein auf gottgleiche Weise, *die gottgleiche Existenz*." This is

[1] Meyer, *l.c.*

contrary to the common elementary rule of grammar that the attributive must be placed between the article and its substantive, not after the latter.

Bishop Lightfoot, taking ἴσα as a predicate, says: "Between the two expressions ἴσος εἶναι and ἴσα εἶναι no other distinction can be drawn, except that the former refers rather to the *person*, the latter to the *attributes*."

This use of the word "*attributes*," without any limitation, seems unfortunately to mar what might otherwise have been a well-drawn distinction. The divine "attributes," properly so-called, are neither really nor formally distinct from the divine essence.[1]

---

[1] Pearson, *De Deo et Attributis*, Lect. iv. p. 39 s. Compare Mansel, *Gnostic Heresies*, p. 182: "These attributes, though manifested to the finite intellect as different, are in their own

The sum of the "attributes" makes up the whole essence; they are therefore inseparable from the very existence of the *person*.

But the term "attributes" may also be used in a relative and less proper sense, of which Bishop Pearson speaks as follows:[1]

"It is also to be observed that from the operations of God in regard to His creatures there arise certain new relations, and from those relations certain titles (*denominationes*) are attributed to God; yet no change can hence be inferred in God, but only in the creatures."

Among such relative attributes we may place the various manifestations of divine power and glory to angels and to men.

nature one with each other, and with the divine essence." See also Newman, *Parochial Sermons*, VI. 378: "All that He is, is Himself, and nothing short of Himself; His attributes are He."

[1] *l.c.* p. 94.

That Bishop Lightfoot was really thinking of these *relative* attributes as indicated by the expression ἴσα εἶναι Θεῷ, is clear from his notes on verse 7 : "'He divested Himself,' not of His divine nature, for this was impossible, but 'of the glories, the prerogatives of Deity'; '*emptied*, stripped *Himself*' of the insignia of majesty." The same interpretation is given on p. 135: "The act expressed by οὐχ ἁρπαγμὸν ἡγήσατο is brought forward as an example of humility, and can only be regarded as such, if the expression τὸ εἶναι ἴσα Θεῷ refers to rights which it was an act of condescension to waive."

Thus the true distinction appears to be that, whereas εἶναι ἴσος would denote equality of nature, εἶναι ἴσα points to the mode of existence, *i.e.* the state and circumstances, or, if the term be preferred, the *relative* attributes, which are separable from the essence, and therefore variable, or, in a logical sense (if we may so speak with reverence), "*accidental.*"

The distinction is the same as that in Latin between the Vulgate, "esse se aequalem Deo," and Tertullian's[1] "pariari Deo," "to be on a par with God," and between "*equal with God*" (A.V.), and "*on an equality with God*" (R.V.).

In opposition to this ancient interpretation Meyer makes the groundless assertion, that because "the emphasis is placed on ἁρπαγμόν, therefore τὸ εἶναι ἴσα Θεῷ cannot be something essentially different from ἐν μορφῇ Θεοῦ ὑπάρχειν, but must in substance denote the same thing, namely, the divine *habitus* of Christ, which is expressed as to

[1] *Adv. Marcion.* v. 20.

its *form of appearance* by ἐν μορφῇ Θεοῦ ὑπάρχων, and as to its internal *nature* by τὸ εἶναι ἴσα Θεῷ."[1]

Again, in the footnote to this passage he adds, that Paul "distinguishes very precisely and suitably between the two ideas representing the same state, by saying that Christ, in His divine pre-human *form of life*, did not venture to use this His God-equal *being* for making booty. Both, therefore, express the very same divine *habitus;* but the εἶναι ἴσα Θεῷ is the general element which presents itself in the divine μορφή as its *substratum* and lies at its basis, so that the two designations *exhaust* the idea of divinity."

We have here two important errors, which introduce a hopeless confusion into Meyer's interpretation.

[1] p. 81, E. Tr.

(1) He uses the word *habitus* to express the whole "idea of divinity," as included and *exhausted* by the two phrases μορφὴ Θεοῦ and εἶναι ἴσα Θεῷ. But this word *habitus*, which Meyer emphasises in both sentences by italics, is the technical Latin for σχῆμα, and is so used both in the Vulgate of v. 7, and in St. Augustine's interpretation of it, "De eo quod scriptum est: *Et habitu inventus ut homo.*"[1]

Meyer himself has given an excellent interpretation of the word in v. 7: "σχῆμα, *habitus*, which receives its more precise reference from the context, denotes here the entire outwardly perceptible mode and form, the whole shape of the phenomenon apparent to the senses (1 Cor. vii. 31). . . . Men saw in Christ a human form, bearing, language, action, mode of life, wants and their satis-

[1] *De diversis Quaestionibus*, lxxiii.

faction, etc., in general the *state and relations* of a human being, so that in the entire mode of His appearance He made Himself known and was recognised (εὑρεθ.) *as a man.*"

(2) Meyer applies ἐν μορφῇ Θεοῦ ὑπάρχων to the "*form of appearance*," and τὸ εἶναι ἴσα Θεῷ to the "internal *nature*" of Christ in His pre-existence. This interpretation is wrong as to both expressions, and actually inverts their meanings.

μορφή, as we have shown above (pp. 26-35), is the "essential form," or "specific character," which pre-supposes the "nature," and is inseparable from it. τὸ εἶναι ἴσα Θεῷ describes the "state and relations" of a Divine Being, His modes of manifestation: it is thus not co-ordinate, but subordinate, to μορφὴ Θεοῦ, just as its correlative in v. 7

"ON AN EQUALITY WITH GOD"

is shown by Meyer himself (p. 90) to be subordinate to μορφὴ δούλου: "The *more precise positive definition* of the *mode* in which He emptied Himself is supplied by μορφὴν δούλου λαβών, and the latter then receives through ἐν ὁμ. ἀνθρ. γενόμενος καὶ σχήματι εὑρ. [ὡς ἄνθρ. *its specification of mode correlative to* εἶναι ἴσα Θεῷ.[1] This specification is not co-ordinate (De Wette, Baumgarten—Crusius, Weiss, Schenkel), but subordinate to μορφὴν δούλου λαβών."

(*b*) The conclusion to which we have just been led by considering the meaning of the words μορφή, σχῆμα, ἴσα Θεῷ, is strongly confirmed by the general structure of vv. 6, 7, and the balance of the two sets of contrasted clauses.

As ἐν μορφῇ Θεοῦ ὑπάρχων finds its antithesis in μορφὴν δούλου λαβών, so οὐχ

[1] The italics are Meyer's own.

ἁρπαγμὸν ἡγήσατο τὸ εἶναι ἴσα Θεῷ is in direct antithesis to ἀλλὰ ἑαυτὸν ἐκένωσεν.

This latter antithetical relation is placed beyond dispute (1) by the direct opposition indicated by οὐκ ... ἀλλά,[1] and (2) by the necessary logical connexion of the two clauses.

For since the phrase ἑαυτὸν ἐκένωσεν conveys of itself an incomplete idea, we are at once driven to ask, Of what did Christ empty himself? And the only possible answer is, He emptied Himself of that which He did not regard as an ἁρπαγμόν. Thus Dr. Bruce (p. 23) says rightly: " Beyond all doubt, therefore, whatever τὸ εἶναι ἴσα Θεῷ may mean, it points to something which both the connexion of thought and the grammatical structure of the sentence require us to regard the Son of God as willing to give up." So Bishop

[1] See below, p. 67.

Westcott on St. John i. 14: *The word was made flesh*, writes: "St. Paul desribes it as an 'emptying of Himself' by the Son of God . . . a laying aside of the mode of divine existence (τὸ εἶναι ἴσα Θεῷ); and this declaration carries us as far as we can go in defining the mystery."

From this again it follows, that τὸ εἶναι ἴσα Θεῷ denotes something which Christ already possessed as "*being in the form of God.*" It is the condition of glory and majesty which was the adequate manifestation of His divine nature, and which He resigned for a time by *taking the form of a servant.*

In order to express the meaning of the clause quite clearly, a slight alteration is required in the Revised Version: *counted it not a prize to be on an equality with God.* The form "*to be*" is ambiguous, and easily lends itself to the erroneous notion that τὸ εἶναι ἴσα Θεῷ was something *to be* acquired in the future. The rendering, *counted it not a prize that He was on an equality with God*, is quite as accurate, and more free from ambiguity.

When De Wette, who acknowledges that "κενοῦν is referred to τὸ εἶναι ἴσα Θεῷ," goes on to say, "and that, in so far as Jesus might have had it in His power, not in that He actually possessed it," Tholuck[1] asks very pertinently, "Who ever employed the word "*empty*" in regard to the renunciation of something *not yet acquired?* Can you say that any one empties himself of that which he does not as yet possess? How much better, with the ancient school of interpreters, to refer κενοῦν to an equality of condition with God actually present, of which Christ resigned the use."

[1] *Disputatio Theologica*, Halle, 1848, p. 14.

De Wette's view, however, is still maintained in the third edition of Thomasius, *Christi Person und Werk*, i. p. 417: "Now if οὐχ ἁρπαγμὸν ἡγήσατο means, as cannot be doubted, *non rapiendum sibi duxit*, τὸ εἶναι ἴσα Θεῷ will mean something which He did *not* possess before, and so something different from μορφὴ Θεοῦ, which belonged to Him as God."

Thomasius names Tholuck as holding this view, although in the passage quoted above from the *Disputatio Theologica* he argues expressly and, as it seems, conclusively against it.

The statements of Thomasius that the meaning "*non rapiendum sibi duxit* cannot be doubted," and that "all other meanings, *non praedam sibi duxit*, or, 'He would not hold it fast pertinaciously,' cannot be justified lexically," are mere arbitrary assertions, which cannot themselves be justified in relation to the context.

We thus get rid of the chief cause of error and confusion in the interpretation of the whole passage, namely, the notion that Christ emptied Himself of "*the form of God.*" This view, though adopted by Meyer, Alford, and other interpreters,[1] is so directly opposed to the meaning of the words, ὑπάρχων, μορφή, ἴσα, Θεῷ, and also to the antithetical arrangement and logical connexion of the several clauses, that I cannot refrain from expressing my firm conviction that it must in the end be regarded

---

[1] Bruce, *Humiliation*, p. 26: "All that can be confidently affirmed is, that the Apostle does conceive the Incarnation under the aspect of an exchange of a divine form for a human form of being: so that, as expositors, we are not entitled to interpret the words, *being in the form of God* as meaning 'continuing to subsist in divine form.'"

as utterly untenable by every competent Greek scholar who will examine the arguments opposed to it carefully, and without dogmatic prejudice.

(c) Assuming, as we now may, that "*the being on an equality with God*" was something which Christ possessed prior to His Incarnation, and then for a time resigned, we have next to consider and choose between two meanings of the word ἁρπαγμόν.

Does it here denote an *action*, a "robbery" (A.V.), or the *object* of an action, "a prize" (R.V.)? In other words, has it an active or a passive signification?

The course of the following inquiry will perhaps be made clearer, if we first show in a free paraphrase the two interpretations to which we are led by the different senses ascribed to ἁρπαγμόν.

1. With the active sense "robbery" or "usurpation" we get the following meaning:

"Who *because* He was subsisting in the essential form of God, did not regard it as any usurpation that He was on an equality of glory and majesty with God, *but yet* emptied Himself of that co-equal glory, by taking the form of a created servant of God."

2. The passive sense gives a different meaning to the passage:

"Who *though* He was subsisting in the essential form of God, *yet* did not regard His being on an equality of glory and majesty with God as a prize and treasure to be held fast, *but* emptied Himself thereof, etc."

Whichever of these interpretations be adopted, the doctrine of the passage in reference to Christ's Person is not affected, so long as we retain the meanings already assigned to μορφὴ Θεοῦ and τὸ εἶναι ἴσα Θεῷ. The interesting point in the discussion of the meanings of ἁρπαγμόν is, which of the two, being otherwise exegetically correct, agrees best with the Apostle's purpose to set forth Christ as the supreme example of humility and self-renunciation.

In favour of the active sense it is urged (1) that this is the meaning of ἁρπαγμός in the only known instance of its use by a classical writer, Plutarch, *de Puerorum Educatione*, p. 12 A τὸν ἐκ Κρήτης καλούμενον ἁρπαγμόν, (2) that the passive sense would be more properly expressed by the very usual form ἅρπαγμα.

Both these arguments are true, but neither of them decisive.

(1) We cannot attach much importance to

the passages quoted by Bishop Lightfoot from Christian writers of the fourth and fifth centuries to show that ἁρπαγμός is equivalent to ἅρπαγμα, because this later usage is probably derived from the very passage before us. But we may fairly say that the single passage from Plutarch, in which the active sense is found, is not sufficient to prove that the word could not have been used in the passive sense in St. Paul's time.

To the arguments urged against the passive sense (2) Bishop Lightfoot replies that " as a matter of fact substantives in -μός are frequently used to describe a concrete thing, e.g. θεσμός, χρησμός, φραγμός, etc."

Of these examples θεσμός and χρησμός are hardly relevant, as these words have no alternative forms in -μα. But φραγμός is a very good instance.

In Herodotus vii. 36, it is applied to the

"fence" or "bulwark" on either side of Xerxes' bridge, constructed to prevent the baggage-animals from seeing the water: φραγμὸν παρείρυσαν ἔνθεν καὶ ἔνθεν.

In Herodotus viii. 52 we read that the Persians, having attached lighted tow to their arrows, ἐτόξευον ἐς τὸ φράγμα, the φράγμα being the barricade of planks and timbers with which the Athenians had tried to fortify the Acropolis.

It is evident that φραγμός in the former passage has the same passive sense as φράγμα in the latter.

This passive sense is also evident in the following passages where φραγμός occurs in the Septuagint and New Testament; Ps. lxxxix. 40; lxii. 4; Prov. xxiv. 31; Is. v. 5; Matt. xxi. 33; Mark xii. 1; Luke xiv. 23; Eph. ii. 14.

Another good example is found in the

usage of σταλαγμός, which, with its cognate σπάλαγμα, exactly corresponds to ἁρπαγμός, ἅρπαγμα.

Thus we read in Aesch. *Eum.* 802:

ἀφεῖσαι δαιμόνων σταλάγματα,

and in Sophocles, *Antig.* 1239:

καὶ φυσιῶν ὀξεῖαν ἐκβάλλει πνοὴν
λευκῇ παρειᾷ φοινίου σταλάγματος.

With these passages compare Aesch. *Theb.* 60:

πεδία δ' ἀργηστὴς ἀφρὸς
χραίνει σταλαγμοῖς ἱππικῶν ἐκ πνευμόνων,

and *Eum.* 246:

τετραυματισμένον γὰρ ὡς κύων νεβρόν,
πρὸς αἷμα καὶ σταλαγμὸν ἐκμαστεύομεν.

Soph. *Fragm.* 340:

λάμπει δ' ἀγνιεὺς βωμὸς ἀτμίζων πυρὶ
σμύρνης σταλαγμούς, βαρβάρους εὐοσμίας.

Eurip. *Ion*, 351:

ἦν δὲ σταλαγμὸς ἐν στίβῳ τις αἵματος;

It is evident that in these latter passages σταλαγμός has exactly the same meaning as στάλαγμα in the former.

While these examples suffice to show that ἁρπαγμός may have a passive sense, its combination with ἡγήσατο renders this probable in the present passage. For Bishop Lightfoot has shown that "with such verbs as ἡγεῖσθαι, ποιεῖσθαι, νομίζειν, etc., ἅρπαγμα is employed like ἕρμαιον, εὕρημα, to denote 'a highly prized possession, an unexpected gain.'"

The two quotations most pertinent, as containing both ἅρπαγμα and ἡγεῖσθαι, are Heliodorus, vii. 20 οὐχ ἅρπαγμα οὐδὲ ἕρμαιον ἡγεῖται τὸ πρᾶγμα, and Titus Bostr. c. *Manich.* i. 2 ἅρπαγμα ψευδῶς τὸ ἀναγκαῖον τῆς φύσεως ἡγεῖται. These passages are both from writers of the fourth century, the only example given from an author nearly contemporary with St. Paul being Plutarch, *de Alexandri Fort.* 330 D οὐδὲ ὥσπερ ἅρπαγμα καὶ λάφυρον εὐτυχίας ἀνελπίστου σπαράξαι καὶ ἀνασύρασθαι διανοηθείς.

We proceed to consider the objections which have been urged by recent commentators against the active sense of ἁρπαγμόν, "usurpation," or "robbery."

(1) One ground of objection has reference to the meaning assigned in this interpretation to ἀλλά, as being virtually equivalent to ἀλλ' ὅμως.

Against this Bishop Ellicott argues very strongly as an undue expansion of the meaning of ἀλλά, and as not retaining "its usual, proper, and logical force after the negative clause."

Bishop Lightfoot also calls this rendering of ἀλλά, "unnatural in itself."

I am not myself disposed to advocate the rendering in the present passage; but with all the deference due to such eminent scholars I venture to think that the expressions used in enforcing their objections are not altogether free from exaggeration.

That ἀλλά is in fact sometimes used by St. Paul in this meaning after a negative clause, cannot well be denied in face of such passages as Romans v. 13: *Sin is not imputed when there is no law. Nevertheless* (ἀλλά) *death reigned, etc.* (R.V.); and 1 Cor. iv. 4: *I know nothing against myself; yet* (ἀλλά) *am I not hereby justified* (R.V.).

On the other hand it must be fully admitted that this sense of ἀλλά after a negative (οὐκ . . . ἀλλά) is very rare in comparison with its more ordinary meaning, "but," expressing a direct contrast to what has gone before.

(2) A second and much more valid objection is based on the relation of οὐχ ἁρπαγμὸν ἡγήσατο to the preceding and following context.

Thus Dr. Martin Routh, commenting on the quotation of Philippians ii. 6, in the *Epistle of the Churches of Vienne and Lyons*, writes as follows:[1] "However the words οὐχ ἁρπαγμὸν ἡγήσατο τὸ εἶναι ἴσα Θεῷ are to be interpreted, this at least is certain, that the Lyonnais drew from them a proof of Christ's humility (τῆς ταπεινοφροσύνης). Nor they alone, but also many other ancient writers did the same; nay more, I will undertake to say that up to the time of the Nicene Council no ecclesiastical writer can be adduced who has clearly and plainly indicated that these words mean, in accordance with the rendering in our English

[1] *Rell. Sacr.* I. p. 364.

Version, 'thought it not a thing alien to Himself.'"

Dr. Routh thus appears to reject the meaning, "He thought it not a robbery but His own by right."

The same objection to the Authorised Version is strongly urged by the ablest of our English commentators, such as Bishop Ellicott, Bishop Lightfoot, and Dean Gwynn in the *Speaker's Commentary*.

They argue with undeniable force

(*a*) that the rendering "thought it not robbery" is *an assertion of rightful dignity*, and that, in a "prominent and emphatic sentence" (Gwynn), where we are led to expect "an instance of self-abnegation or humility," exemplifying the principle in v. 4, *not looking each to his own things, but each also to the things of others*.

"We expect this appeal to our great

Example (v. 5) to be followed immediately by a reference, not to the right which He *claimed*, but to the dignity which He renounced. . . . The mention of our Lord's condescension is thus postponed too late in the sentence" (Lightfoot).

(*b*) A further objection is thus stated by Dean Gwynn : "The following verse (7), describing the act by which He 'emptied Himself,' brings it into the sharpest contrast by the introductory '*but*' (ἀλλά, *i.e.* 'but on the contrary,' as in vv. 3, 4) with that which is conveyed by the verb (ἡγήσατο) of this sentence. But 'to think it robbery to be equal with God' stands in no such contrast with 'to empty Himself.' To say 'He did not count it a wrongful act to assert Divine Attributes (?), but *on the contrary* laid them aside,' is unmeaning."

Admitting the force of these arguments,

we believe the right meaning of the clause to be that the Son of God did not regard His being on equal conditions of glory and majesty with God as a prize and treasure to be held fast, but emptied Himself thereof, becoming thus the supreme example of that willing self-sacrifice for the good of others, which is the aim of the Apostle's exhortation.

Before passing on, we may do well to observe the perfect accuracy with which St. Paul applies the verbs ὑπάρχειν, εἶναι, and γίγνεσθαι, the first to the eternal *subsistence* of "the form of God," the second to states and conditions *existing at a particular time*, but presently to be laid aside, and the last (γενόμενον) to *the entrance upon a new existence* "in the likeness of men."

vi. Passing to the next clause, ἀλλὰ ἑαυτὸν ἐκένωσεν, we observe that—

(1) The position of ἑαυτόν before ἐκένωσεν lays an emphasis upon the thought that the self-emptying was Christ's own voluntary act, an act corresponding to the precept in v. 4 μὴ τὰ ἑαυτῶν ἕκαστοι σκοποῦντες, and strongly contrasted with the idea of ἁρπαγμόν in v. 6.

"Where," exclaims Chrysostom, "are those who say that He was under constraint and made subject? *Himself He emptied*, says the Scripture, *Himself He humbled.*"[1]

(2) The verb κενόω is sometimes followed by a Genitive denoting "*the contents*" which are removed, as in Plato, *Republ.* viii. 560 D τούτων . . . κενώσαντες τὴν . . . ψυχήν.

Sympos. 197 C οὗτος . . . ἡμᾶς ἀλλοτριότητος κενοῖ.

And Plutarch, *Apophth. Lacon.* 229 D τὰν ψυχὰν κενῶσαι κακῶν.

[1] Compare p. 151.

When, as in *Phil.* ii. 7, there is no Genitive expressed, the idea of *the contents* must be gathered from the context; and in this case the antithetical relation between τὸ εἶναι ἴσα Θεῷ and ἑαυτὸν ἐκένωσεν, enforced as it is by the *direct* contradiction οὐκ . . . ἀλλά, leaves no room for doubt.

Accordingly the only admissible interpretation is that which was given by the Synod of Antioch (A.D. 269) in the *Epistle to Paul of Samosata* before his deposition,[1] οὗ χάριν ὁ αὐτὸς Θεὸς καὶ ἄνθρωπος Ἰησοῦς Χριστὸς . . . ἐν τῇ ἐκκλησίᾳ τῇ ὑπὸ τὸν οὐρανὸν πάσῃ πεπίστευται Θεὸς μὲν κενώσας ἑαυτὸν ἀπὸ τοῦ εἶναι ἴσα Θεῷ, ἄνθρωπος δὲ καὶ ἐκ σπέρματος Δαβὶδ τὸ κατὰ σάρκα.

"On which account the same God and man Jesus Christ in all the Church under heaven has been believed in as God having

[1] Cf. Routh, *Rell. Sacr.* tom. iii. p. 298.

emptied Himself from being on an equality with God, and as man of the seed of David according to the flesh." [1]

When Meyer asserts (p. 88) that Christ "emptied *Himself*, and that, as the context places beyond doubt, of the *divine* μορφή, which He possessed, but now exchanged for a μορφὴ δούλου," he simply repeats, with ill-founded confidence, that identification, or, rather we may say, confusion of μορφὴ Θεοῦ with τὸ εἶναι ἴσα Θεῷ, which has been shown above (pp. 52 f.) to be the chief cause of so much erroneous interpretation of the passage.

VII. In the next clause (μορφὴν δούλου λαβών) the action of the participle λαβών, as also of the following γενόμενος, coincides in time with that of the verb ἐκένωσεν. The state of glory and majesty implied in

[1] Compare p. 153.

the being on an equality with God was laid aside in the act of *taking the form of a servant, being made in the likeness of men.* It is undeniable that this coincidence in time between the verb and its participles necessarily fixes the action of ἐκένωσεν at the first moment of the Incarnation, and excludes all attempts, such as those of Luther and his followers, to assign it to any later period of Christ's human life.[1]

On the meaning of "*servant*" in this passage, Bishop Lightfoot writes: "For ἄνθρωπος the stronger word δοῦλος is substituted: He, who is Master (κύριος) of all, became the slave of all. Comp. Matt. xx. 27, 28; Mark x. 44, 45."

But this reference of δοῦλος is decisively rejected by Bishop Bull, *Primitive Tradition on the Deity of Christ*, vi. 21, a passage

[1] See p. 110 ff.

briefly referred to by Bishop Ellicott: "It is to be observed that *the form of a servant* by no means signifies here a servile condition of man, in as far as it is opposed to the state and condition of a man who is free and his own master, as the heretics contend, and some Catholics have imprudently admitted. For *the form of a servant* is here manifestly contrasted with *the form of God.* And in comparison with God every creature has the form of a servant, and is bound to obedience towards God. Hence the Apostle . . . presently adds γενόμενος ὑπήκοος, *became obedient*, namely, to God the Father."[1]

Bishop Pearson is equally emphatic in rejecting this reference to human slavery: "It is a vain imagination that our Saviour then first appeared a servant, when He was

[1] See also *Def. Fid. Nic.* P. i. L. ii. c. 2, § 2.

apprehended, bound, scourged, crucified. . . . Our Saviour in all the degrees of His humiliation never lived as a servant unto any master on earth."

The full significance of the title, *form of a servant*, is explained at great length by Dean Jackson in his admirable *Commentaries upon the Apostles' Creed*, bk. viii. capp. 7ff., where he argues that when Christ "did in the fulness of time take our nature upon Him, He did wholly submit His reasonable will, all His affections and desires, unto the will of His Heavenly Father: and in this renouncing of the arbitrament of His will, and in the entire submission of it unto the will of His Father, did that *form of a servant*, whereof our Apostle speaks, formally consist."

The true meaning of μορφή in the expression *form of God* is confirmed by its recurrence in the corresponding phrase, *form of a servant.*

It is universally admitted that the two phrases are directly antithetical, and that "*form*" must therefore have the same sense in both.

The argument to be drawn from this acknowledged fact is well expressed by Chrysostom in his Commentary on the Epistle: "What then should we say in answer to Arius, who said that the Son is of other substance (than the Father)? Tell me, what is the meaning of this—'*He took the form of a servant*'? He became man, says Arius. Therefore also *subsisting in the form of God*, He was God. For the word used in both places is μορφή. If the one (μορφὴ δούλου) is true, the other is true: *the form of a servant*, man by nature; therefore *the form of God*, God by nature."

IS ST. PAUL'S LANGUAGE INEXACT? 79

It is sometimes asserted that in taking *the form of a servant* it was necessary to be divested of *the form of God;* in other words, that the two natures in their fulness and perfection could not exist together in one Person.[1]

Thus Canon Gore [2] writes, " The question has been asked, Does St. Paul imply that Jesus Christ abandoned the μορφὴ Θεοῦ ? " And his answer is, " I think all we can certainly say is that He is conceived to have emptied Himself of the divine mode of existence (μορφή) so far as was involved in His really entering upon the human mode of existence. St. Paul does not use his terms with the exactness of a professional logician or scholastic."[3]

---

[1] See above, p. 24.

[2] *Dissertations on subjects connected with the Incarnation*, pp. 88 f.

[3] In like manner Canon Gore's Reviewer in

I have always found it dangerous to assume that St. Paul was inexact in his use of language, especially in passages which have an important doctrinal significance; and I have been led by frequent experience to the conclusion that the fault lay in my own want of a clear perception of the Apostle's meaning, and not in any vagueness of expression on his part.

Such, I believe, is the cause of Canon Gore's difficulty in the present instance.

He has not grasped the true meaning of μορφὴ Θεοῦ, and the distinction between it and τὸ εἶναι ἴσα Θεῷ. This is very evident in the following passage, in which the italics are mine, and are meant to call attention to the uncertainty of Canon Gore's

The Guardian, 1st January 1896, says that "St. Paul must have been using the word 'form' in a loose popular sense, as we use the word 'nature.'"

interpretation, and his confusion of the two phrases. "The word 'form,' transferred from physical shape to spiritual type, describes—as St. Paul uses it, alone or in composition, with uniform accuracy — *the permanent characteristics* of a thing. Jesus Christ then, in His pre-existent state, was living in the permanent characteristics of *the life* of God.

"In such a life it was His right to remain. It belonged to Him.

"But He regarded not His *prerogatives* as a man regards a prize he must clutch at. For love of us he abjured *the prerogatives of equality with God.*

"By an act of deliberate self-abnegation, He so emptied Himself as to assume *the permanent characteristics* of the human or servile life."

Now though St. Paul, we have been told above, "does not use his terms with the exactness of a professional logician or scholastic," yet μορφή must be an exception, for here we are told that he uses it "with uniform accuracy." First then it describes "*the permanent characteristics of a thing*," that is, in this case, "the permanent characteristics" of God; then, with a slight but not unimportant modification, "the permanent characteristics of the *life* of God"; then, with a further change, it means "prerogatives," and so at last "the prerogatives of *equality with God.*" When we add to this series of transformations Canon Gore's previous definition of μορφὴ Θεοῦ as "the divine mode of existence," we certainly find a great want of "exactness," which cannot, however, be laid to the charge of the Apostle.

The same mode of dealing with our passage was adopted by Schleiermacher, who, as Dr. Bruce very justly remarks (p. 19), sought " to deprive the statements contained therein of all theological value, by representing them as of an 'ascetic' and 'rhetorical' character; the expressions not being intended to be 'didactically fixed,'—a convenient method of getting rid of unacceptable theological dogmas, which may be applied to any extent, and which, if applied to St. Paul's Epistles, would render it difficult to extract any theological inferences therefrom, inasmuch as nearly all the doctrinal statements they contain arise out of a practical occasion, and are intended to serve a hortatory purpose."

VIII. In the following clause the meaning of *taking the form of a servant* is more closely defined by the words ἐν ὁμοιώματι ἀνθρώπων γενόμενος, *being made in the likeness of men.*

The relation of this clause to the preceding is well stated by Bishop Bull, *Primitive Tradition*, vi. 21 : " Christ took *the form of a servant* at the time when He was made man. This is clear from those words of the Apostle, ἑαυτὸν ἐκένωσε, μορφὴν δούλου λαβών, ἐν ὁμοιώματι ἀνθρώπων γενόμενος, in which there is a continuous ἐξήγησις, whereby the latter clause is subjoined to the former immediately (ἀμέσως,), without the interposition of any copulative conjunction. If you ask how Christ emptied Himself, the Apostle answers, *by taking the form of a servant.* If you ask again, how Christ took the form of a servant, the answer follows immediately, *being made in the likeness of men*, that is, being made man, like unto us men, sin only excepted."

So Bishop Pearson, referring to the Authorised Version, writes: "Our translation of that verse is not only not exact, but very disadvantageous to the truth which is contained in it. For we read it thus: *He made Himself of no reputation and took upon Him the form of a servant, and was made in the likeness of men.* Where we have two copulative conjunctions, neither of which is in the original text, and three distinct propositions, without any dependence of one upon the other; whereas all the words together are but an expression of Christ's exinanition, with an explication showing in what it consisteth: which will clearly appear by this literal translation, *But emptied Himself, taking the form of a servant, being made in the likeness of men.* Where if any man doubt how Christ emptied Himself, the text will satisfy him, by *taking the form of a servant;* if any still question how He took the form of a servant, he hath the Apostle's resolution, by *being made in the likeness of men*. Indeed, after the expression of this exinanition, he goes on with a conjunction, to add another act of Christ's humiliation: *And being found in fashion as a man, He humbled Himself,* etc. etc."

This excellent exposition stands in strong contrast to Meyer's fanciful attempt to maintain a different construction of the clauses: "The division, by which a stop is placed before καὶ σχήματι εὑρεθεὶς ὡς ἄνθρωπος, is at variance with the purposely-chosen expressions σχήματι and εὑρεθείς, both of which correspond to the idea of μορφή, and thereby show that καὶ σχήματι εὑρεθεὶς ὡς ἄνθρωπος is still a portion of the modal definition of μορφὴν δούλου λαβών."

The expression *likeness of men* does not of itself necessarily imply, still less does it exclude or diminish, the reality of the nature which Christ assumed. That, as we have seen, is declared in the words *form of a servant.* "Paul justly says: ἐν ὁμοιώματι ἀνθρώπων, because, in fact, Christ, although certainly perfect man (Rom. v. 15 ; 1 Cor. xv. 21 ; 1 Tim. ii. 5), was, by reason of the divine nature present in Him not *simply and merely* man, not a *purus putus homo*, but the *Incarnate Son of God.*"[1]

We thus see that the full and proper meaning of μορφή is not less essential to the doctrine of Christ's true humanity than to that of His perfect deity, as presented in this passage.

The plural ἀνθρώπων is used because Christ's humanity represented that which is by nature common to all men. Thus Hooker,

[1] Meyer, after Theophylact and Chrysostom: compare Fritzsche, *Rom.* viii. 3.

E.P. v. cap. 52, § 3, writes: "It pleased not the Word or Wisdom of God to take to itself some one person among men, for then should that one have been advanced which was assumed and no more, but Wisdom, to the end she might save many, built her house of that Nature which is common unto all; she made not *this or that man* her habitation, but dwelt *in us*."

IX. The next participial clause καὶ σχήματι εὑρεθεὶς ὡς ἄνθρωπος, belonging to the following verb ἐταπείνωσεν, declares what Christ appeared to be in the eyes of men, and so prepares the way for the statement of that further humiliation to which He submitted at their hands. As μορφή and ὁμοίωμα describe what He was in Himself as Man, so σχῆμα denotes the entire outwardly perceptible mode and shape of His existence.

This meaning is well brought out by Meyer: "Men saw in Christ a human form, bearing, language, action, mode of life, wants and their satisfaction, etc., in general the *state and relations* of a human being, so that in the entire mode of His appearance He made Himself known and was recognised (εὑρεθείς) *as a man*."

The clause gives no real support to the docetic view of Christ's humanity, which Marcion[1] of old, and Baur in modern times (*Paul*, ii. p. 52, E. Tr.) tried to find in it, but rather implies the contrary. In the whole mode and fashion of His life, in every sensible proof whereby a man is recognised and known *as man*, Christ was so recognised and known and *found as man*.

x. The words *He humbled Himself* mark

[1] Tertullian, *c. Marcion.* v. cap. 20. See more on this point below, pp. 105 f.

a distinct and further step in that self-humiliation which began when He emptied Himself of His Godlike majesty and glory. Both acts were voluntary (as is expressly shown by the use of the word ἑαυτόν in each case), both sprang from the same mind and spirit of loving self-sacrifice, and both were accompanied by the same self-consciousness of deity,[1] which is implied in the fact that, as is shown above, He was still *subsisting in the form of God*. It is this continuous self-consciousness of the Son of God that gives the true measure of His transcendent humility, in every act of submission to His Father's will, in suffering patiently endured, in man's ingratitude meekly borne, and finally in

---

[1] Meyer, p. 97 (E. Trs.): "The self-consciousness of Christ necessarily remained the self-consciousness of the Son of God developing Himself humanly."

obedience *unto death, even the death of the cross.*

XI. vv. 9-11. The extreme and final depth of Christ's self-humiliation in submitting to His shameful death finds its immediate and necessary reward in an exaltation proportionately great. Thus the Apostle's exhortation to the Philippians to *have the same mind which was also in Christ Jesus* is finally enforced by the promise of a glorious reward for themselves, which, though not expressed, is necessarily implied in this supreme fulfilment of the divine law that *he that humbleth himself shall be exalted.*

It is important to observe that this exaltation applies to Christ primarily and properly in His human nature only. This distinction was carefully maintained by Athanasius and other Fathers against the

Arians, who, denying the eternal generation of the Son, argued from the "*wherefore*" in this passage, that, being exalted as the reward of His work on earth, Christ was "therefore called both Son and God, without being very Son."[1] To this Athanasius replies that, "As Christ died and was exalted as man, so, as man, is He said to receive what, as God, He ever had, that even such a grant of grace might reach unto us."[2] "For as He was ever worshipped as being the Word, and *subsisting in the form of God*, so being the same, and having become man, and been called Jesus, He none the less has the whole creation under foot and bending their knees to Him in His Name, and confessing that the Word's becoming flesh, and undergoing death in flesh, has not happened against the glory of His Godhead, but ' *to the*

---

[1] Athan. *c. Arian.* i. § 37.   [2] § 42.

glory of the Father.' For it is the Father's glory that man, made and then lost, should be found again; and when dead, that he should be made alive, and should become God's temple." [1]

Dean Jackson, however, shows [2] that, in a certain sense, even the Divine nature is exalted, not in itself but in relation to us, by the "glorious attributes of being our Lord and Redeemer, and of being the Fountain of grace and salvation unto us.

"All these are real attributes, and suppose a real ground or foundation; and that was, *His humbling Himself unto death, even unto the death of the cross.* Nor are these attributes only real, but more glorious, both in respect of God the Father, who was pleased to give His only Son for us, and in respect of God the Son, who was pleased to pay our

---

[1] § 42. [2] *On the Creed*, bk. XI. c. ii. § 4.

ransom by His humiliation, than the attribute of creation is.

"The Son of God, then, not the Son of David only, hath been exalted since His death to be our Lord, by a new and real title, by the title of redemption and salvation. This is the sum of our Apostle's inference concerning our Saviour's exaltation, Phil. ii. 11: *That every tongue should confess that Jesus Christ is Lord, to the glory of God the Father.*"

In τὸ ὄνομα the article, which has been rightly restored by the Revisers on the united authority of ℵ A B C, is full of significance. We know what "the Name" meant to every Hebrew, and St. Paul was *a Hebrew of the Hebrews*. To him "the Name which is above every name" could mean nothing less than the sacred Name, Jehovah. This meaning seems to be placed beyond doubt, when we see that St. Paul immediately quotes the great passage, Is. xlv. 23: *By myself have I sworn . . . that unto Me every knee shall bow, every tongue shall swear.*

Bishop Lightfoot observes that, "If St. Paul were referring to any one term, Κύριος would best explain the reference, for it occurs in the context ὅτι Κύριος Ἰησοῦς Χριστός." Now Κύριος is the constant rendering of the Name יהוה, and thus the Apostle's meaning is clearly seen to be, that He who says in Isaiah (v. 18) *I am the Lord; and there is none else*, graciously *gave* (ἐχαρίσατο) *to Him*, the son of Man (Lightfoot), the Name which He gives to no other.

There is a very interesting comment on our passage in Jeremy Taylor's *Life of Christ*, Part i. § 5, 8; "Because God gave to the Holy Babe the name in which the treasures of mercy were deposited, and exalted 'this name above all names,' we are taught that the purpose of His counsel was, to exalt and magnify His mercy above all His other works; He being delighted with this excellent demonstration of it in the mission and manifestation and crucifixion of His Son, hath changed the ineffable name into a name utterable by man, and desirable by all the world; the majesty is all arrayed in robes of mercy, the *tetragrammaton*, or adorable mystery of the patriarchs, is made fit for pronunciation and expression, when it becometh the name of the Lord's Christ." Compare *Orac. Sibyll.* i. 324-327, and Dr. C. Taylor's note in the new edition of *Sayings of the Jewish Fathers* on the custom of bowing at the name of God.

We may now look back for a moment on the results of our interpretation, so far as they affect the inferences that may, or may not, rightly be drawn from the passage in regard to the Person and Natures of Christ in His state of humiliation.

1. We have seen that the word ὑπάρχων, *subsisting*, as used by St. Paul, denotes both the pre-existence and the continued existence of Christ *in the form of God;* pp. 8–21.

2. In illustration and confirmation of Bishop Lightfoot's interpretation of the word μορφή as "essential form," it has been shown that this sense was well known to contemporaries of St. Paul, that it was adopted generally by the early Greek Fathers, and advisedly restored to our English Bible by the Translators of the Authorised Version in A.D. 1611; pp. 22–36.

3. We have noticed briefly the opposite theory of those who contend that the *form*

is separable from the *nature* and *essence*, that they can exist without it, and that in the Incarnation the Son of God did in fact empty Himself of the *form*, while retaining the essential nature, of deity. This error will be further discussed and traced to its source in certain false definitions of Zanchi, pp. 122 ff., where it will be more fully shown that the Son could not possibly empty Himself of the *form* of God without thereby ceasing to be God in any true sense.

4. Next we have seen that ἴσα Θεῷ denotes the manifold circumstances of glory and majesty, or the particular modes of manifestation, which were an adequate expression of the divine nature of the Son, but not inseparable from it, pp. 37-58.

5. It has been seen that the meaning of the clause οὐχ ἁρπαγμὸν ἡγήσατο τὸ εἶναι

ἴσα Θεῷ, and its direct antithesis to ἀλλ᾽ ἑαυτὸν ἐκένωσε, clearly prove that what the Son of God laid aside at the Incarnation was that equality of conditions, such as glory, majesty, and honour, which He possessed in His pre-existent state, and to which He prayed to be restored, in John xvii. 5 : *And now, O Father, glorify Thou Me with Thine own self, with the glory which I had with Thee before the world was*, pp. 59-74.

6. We have seen how the Apostle sets forth on the other hand the fulness of Christ's humanity in a climax advancing from its most general to its most special features,—from that *form of a servant* which includes all God's creatures as *ministers of His who do His pleasure*,—to that *likeness of men* which unites Him with us in our true nature as made *in the image of God*,—and finally to

that outward guise and fashion, in which He was seen as a *man of sorrows and acquainted with grief*, humbling Himself yet further in obedience to His Father's will unto death, even the death of the cross, pp. 75-90.

St. Paul has thus shown us in brief outline the essential features of the Incarnation, the perfect Godhead and perfect Manhood united in the one Divine Person, who is the subject of the whole passage, and "never to be divided," seeing that the Human nature, denoted in the name Jesus, is now highly exalted in inseparable union with the Divine, pp. 91-96.

But as to the manner in which those two natures are united in one Person,—as to the degree in which the Deity was limited or the Humanity exalted by their union, *during*

Christ's life on earth, the Apostle has said nothing whatever in this passage.

In fact, the precise manner of this union has been justly described by one of the best English divines of a former age as "a mystery the most to be admired by all, and least possible to be expressed by any living man, of all the mysteries whose belief we profess in the Apostles' Creed, the mystery of the Blessed Trinity alone excepted."[1]

If then the conclusions warranted by the language of St. Paul leave much still unexplained and incomprehensible to man's understanding in the mystery of Christ's Holy Incarnation, they may yet be justly said to reveal as much as is needed for the confirmation of our faith.

The continuance in Christ of *the form of God* assures us that at least the moral

[1] Jackson, *On the Creed,* vii. c. 30.

attributes of the Godhead are faithfully represented in the one perfect image of the Father, His Incarnate Word. And thus His every act of tender compassion, of patient endurance, and of loving self-sacrifice shines out in its perfect beauty as a revelation of God's own nature, and of His gracious disposition towards us.

If, on the other hand, the *form of God* is laid aside in *taking the form of a servant*, and the influence of the Divine nature thus suppressed, as in kenotic theories, the life of Christ on earth may still serve for our example, by showing what *man* may possibly attain when endued with the fulness of grace and power by the Holy Spirit; but by ceasing to be a direct revelation of the character of God it loses the power "to clothe eternal love with breathing life."[1]

[1] Hutton, *Theological Essays*, p. 289.

PART II

NOTES ON THE HISTORY OF THE INTERPRETATION

PART II

NOTES ON THE HISTORY OF THE INTERPRETATION.

APPARENTLY the earliest attempt to misrepresent the meaning of the Apostle's words was that of Marcion (*c.* A.D. 150), directed against the reality of Christ's human nature.

"Of course," writes Tertullian,[1] "the Marcionites suppose that they have the Apostle on their side in the following passage in the matter of Christ's substance —that in Him there was nothing but a phantom of flesh. For he says of Christ that "subsisting in the form of God, He thought

[1] *Adversus Marcionem*, V. c. 20.

it not robbery to be on equality with God, but emptied Himself, by taking upon Him the *form* of a servant," *not the reality*, " and was made in the *likeness* of man," *not a man*, "and was found in *fashion* as a man," *not in substance*, that is to say, flesh ; just as if there were not also a substance to which *fashion* and *likeness* and *form* are attached."

Dr. F. C. Baur employs the same argument to prove that the Epistle to the Philippians could not be a genuine work of St. Paul. After finding supposed evidence of Gnostic modes of thought and expression in ἁρπαγμόν, ἐκένωσεν, μορφὴ Θεοῦ, and μορφὴ δούλου, he proceeds as follows.[1]

" In a writer so obviously influenced by Gnostic ideas, it cannot surprise us to find a close approach to the Docetism of the

[1] Baur, *Paul, his Life and Works*, vol. ii. pp. 51 ff.

Gnostics. This is undoubtedly the case in verse 7. If, as ἐν ὁμοιώματι ἀνθρώπων γενόμενος, Christ was only ὅμοιος to men, then He was no true and actual man, but only seemed to be so. The expression ὁμοίωμα can signify only similarity, analogy; it cannot denote identity or parity of essence." . . . "That this is the meaning of ὁμοίωμα in our passage is sufficiently clear from the phrase σχήματι εὑρεθεὶς ὡς ἄνθρωπος, which stands close beside it, and does not admit of any other interpretation." . . . "In σχῆμα we have, as clearly as need be, the notion of an *externus habitus*, of a thing changing, passing, and quickly disappearing (cf. 1 Cor. vii. 31)."

Dr. Bruce says in reply to this, that "while it may not be impossible to put a doketic construction on the letter of the passage, such a construction is utterly excluded by its spirit"; and that "from the mind in which the Incarnation took its origin, the complete likeness of Christ's humanity to ours may be inferred with great confidence. He who was not minded to retain His equality with God, was not likely to assume a humanity that was a make-believe or a sham."[1]

This inference from the "*spirit*" of the passage is true in itself, but hardly conclusive; and it is much more satisfactory to be able to show that Dr. Baur's charge of Docetism is entirely excluded by the actual words of the Apostle. While commenting carefully on the subordinate terms ὁμοίωμα and σχῆμα, Dr. Baur omits here all mention of the more important expression μορφὴ δούλου: yet this, *by his own showing*, must exclude all idea of an imperfect or transient

[1] *l.c.* p. 31.

condition, for he says elsewhere that, "If Christ was ἐν μορφῇ Θεοῦ ὑπάρχων, then His nature was from this very fact divine."[1]

A great part of the confusion which has been introduced into the interpretation of our passage had its source in the use made by Erasmus of a passage in the *Commentary on the Epistles of St. Paul* by an unknown author surnamed Ambrosiaster or Pseudo-Ambrosius, from his work having been falsely attributed to St. Ambrose.

Ambrosiaster wrote that "Christ was always in the form of God, because He is the image of the invisible God. But the Apostle is speaking of the Son of God when He was incarnate and made man. . . . When He dwelt among men, it was evident by His words and works that He was God.

[1] *Theol. Jahrb.* viii. 508 *sq.*, quoted by the Editor of Baur's *Paulus*, II. p. 49.

For the form of God differs in nothing from God."

Upon this Erasmus founds the following disingenuous statement: "St. Ambrose interprets form as a specimen or example, because when walking in a human body He yet gave proofs of divinity. For what," says he, "is the form of God but an example, because he appears as God, while He wakes the dead, gives hearing to the deaf, cleanses the lepers.

". . . Accordingly this whole passage seems to me to be violently perverted when applied to Christ's nature, whereas Paul is speaking of the appearance exhibited to us."[1]

This opinion of Erasmus, that the whole passage refers only to Christ's human life, was unhappily adopted by Luther; for as Dr. Dorner observes, "The words of Phil.

[1] Erasmus, *Annotationes in Nov. Test.*

ii. 6 ff., as is well known, are referred by him not to the deity but to the humanity, and his example has been followed by Lutheran dogmaticians."[1]

The effect on the *exegesis* of the passage has thus been permanent and disastrous; but it would be unjust to infer that either Luther himself, or Lutherans in general, have adopted all the doctrinal consequences which would logically follow from their exegesis.

To avoid misrepresentation, it will be best to adopt the words of Dr. Dorner, who thus describes Luther's discussion with Hier. von Dungersheim in the year 1519.[2] "The figure or form of God is not the *essence* of

---

[1] Dorner, *Person of Christ*, Dic. II. vol. ii. p. 96. Compare *System of Christian Doctrine*, iii. 238.

[2] Dorner, *Person of Christ*, II. ii. p. 391.

God; for, in the first place, Christ did not lay down nor renounce the divine essence; nor, in the second place, did He assume the *essence*, but merely the appearance and form of a servant. As to His inner being He continued to be a free Son. "Form," however, must in both cases be taken in the same signification. By the "Form of God," therefore, we must understand the wisdom, might, righteousness, piety, and freedom of the God-Man. The sense we arrive at, consequently, is the following:— Christ was man, free, powerful, wise, subject to no one, excellent in those forms which chiefly befit God. Nevertheless, He was not haughty in this form; He did not act disdainfully towards others who were servants, nor did He regard as a robbery that which He was; He did not presumptuously attribute or assume this form to Himself, but attributed and gave it up to God, and for Himself renounced and laid it down, not wishing to be unlike us, but determining to become as one of us."

... ".Dungersheim appealed to the circumstance, that the passage had always been used in proof of the deity of the Son, to which Luther replied: The fathers have often enough erred; it is enough that we do not cause them to be pronounced heretics; the Scripture is not to be interpreted and judged through them, but they through the Scriptures. Even though he should grant that the passage may be mediately referred to the deity, still it is more fitting to refer it to the humanity of Christ. Referred to the humanity alone, we arrive at a real abasement of Christ; otherwise not, seeing that the deity cannot, strictly speaking, be abased."

For an explanation of the doctrinal results of this interpretation, the reader may refer to Dorner, *l.c.* pp. 81, 95. Our present concern is with the interpretation itself, and in this it is evident that Luther is acting upon his own advice, "*to utter the new wisdom as in new tongues*"; for the Apostle's words are so transformed as to assume a wholly new meaning. Thus μορφὴ Θεοῦ is not the divine essence; ὑπάρχων has no reference to the pre-existence of the co-eternal Son, but to some undefined period in Christ's human life, at which He renounced for Himself and gave up to God those attributes of the God-Man "which chiefly befit God," and so are denoted by "the form of God." At this same undefined period He took "*the form of a servant, being made in the likeness of men*"; from which we must conclude that between the times of His

Incarnation and this exinanition He had not *been made in the likeness of men.* The μορφὴ δούλου which He assumed was not the *essence*, but merely the *appearance* and form of a servant.

Can we wonder, at this point, that Melanchthon was afraid that Luther's view would lead to Docetism, and exclaimed "Marcion is breaking into your house (*will dir in Garten*)."[1]

The interpretation of the whole passage was thus thrown into inextricable confusion, the true meaning of the most important words perverted, and every safeguard against the intrusion of the Eutychian and Docetic heresies recklessly thrown aside.

[1] Dorner, *Hist. Protest. Theol.* i. p. 326. Compare *Bruce*, *l.c.* p. 140: "The Lutheran Christology, to say the least, threatens with extinction the reality of Christ's human nature."

Calvin's interpretation of μορφὴ Θεοῦ was no better than Luther's. In his commentary on the epistle he writes: "*The form of God* here signifies majesty. For just as a man is known from beholding his form, so the majesty, which shines in God, is the figure of Himself. Or if you would prefer an apter simile, the form of a king is the apparel and splendour which indicates the king, as sceptre, diadem, cloak, apparitors, tribunal, and the other ensigns of royalty; the form of a consul is a toga bordered with purple, an ivory chair, lictors with rods and axes. Christ, therefore, before the creation of the world was in the form of God, because He was in possession of His glory from the beginning with the Father, as John says, xvii. 5."

It will be seen as we proceed that the meanings thus assigned by Luther and

Calvin to μορφὴ Θεοῦ belong not to it but to τὸ εἶναι ἴσα Θεῷ.

A striking proof of the permanent, and mischievous effect of Luther's misinterpretation may be found in Dr. Dorner's own treatment of the passage.

Dr. Dorner himself has been justly described as "one of the greatest modern divines and teachers of Germany," and again as "one of the profoundest and most learned theologians of the nineteenth century:"[1] and probably no foreign author of our day has exercised a more powerful and, in some respects, beneficial influence on English theology. We may add that Dr. Dorner was also one of the most earnest and devout representatives of Lutheran orthodoxy; and in the interpretation of our passage he followed only

[1] *Schaff-Herzog Encyclopaedia*, Appendix.

too faithfully the guidance of the great Reformer.

"Paul does not prefix 'Christ,' but 'Jesus Christ' as subject. Consequently there is no necessity present for the reference of the humiliation to the Divine side for the end of the Incarnation.

"An example must be historically cognisable, which that supposed invisible and transcendent act of a self-emptying of the eternal Son prior to the Incarnation would not be.

"The passage will therefore be better translated, that Jesus Christ although in divine *outline or form*, and thereby being already in *the likeness of God* (ἐν μ. Θ. ὑπ.), held equality with God (τὸ εἶναι . . Θεῷ), which is supposed to pertain to Him *as the God-human unity*, to be no fact of an arbitrary or powerful snatching for oneself, to be no robbery, which He has to drag to Himself of His own might, but in complete self-forgetfulness and humiliation He showed His humble and self-forgetful life of love."[1]

It is evident that this interpretation is opposed on every important point to that which we have tried to set forth as required by the usual principles of grammar, and by the true meaning of the Apostle's words.

ὑπάρχων no longer denotes an existence prior to the time of the Incarnation. μορφὴ Θεοῦ instead of the *essential* form of God is no more than a *divine outline or form*, a *likeness of God;* τὸ εἶναι ἴσα Θεῷ instead of the glory which the Word had

[1] *System of Christian Doctrine,* iii. p. 182, 183.

with the Father before the world was, and resigned on becoming Man, is an equality with God, which was not originally His own, but pertains to Him as the God-Man.

The Person of the Incarnate Son is no longer the Divine Person of the Eternal Son, but a Divine-Human personality which first comes into existence with the union of the two natures.

Yet Dorner admits that "the logical consequence of the Lutheran theory" is "a real God-manhood, pre-existent, and the cause of the humanity, whose existence began with the conception."[1]

It is no part of our purpose to trace the various forms which Luther's Christology assumed in the hands of his followers, nor

[1] Bruce, p. 147: Dorner, *Person of Christ*, II. vol. ii. 292-297 (and 247), 431-5.

the contrast between it and the doctrines held by Melanchthon, Zwingli, Calvin, and the Reformed Church in general. Dr. Bruce's lucid and impartial treatment of these and similar points in the history of these doctrines will be found at least as interesting and intelligible as the more voluminous works of Dorner and other German theologians.

Our concern is with matters which have materially affected the exegesis of the passage before us; and in this connexion we need only name the treatise of the Lutheran Chemnitz, *De duabus in Christo Personis* 1570, as having in turn called forth on the side of the Reformed Church the work of Lambert Daneau, "Examen libri *De duabus in Christo Naturis* a Chemnitió conscripti." Genev. 1581.

In this work Daneau seems to have introduced¹ certain novel definitions of οὐσία, φύσις, and μορφή.

Zanchi, another member of the Reformed Church, and Professor of Divinity at Strasburg (1553), and at Heidelberg (1568), in his elaborate and learned *Commentary on the Epistle to the Philippians*, and again in his work *De Incarnatione Filii Dei*, adopted Daneau's definitions, which are as follows:—

"οὐσία properly signifies the bare essence, which is usually expressed by the definition made up of *genus* and *difference*, by which (according to Aristole's doctrine) the τὸ τί ἦν εἶναι is declared: *e.g.* the οὐσία of man is to be an animal endowed with reason. For this is the proper definition of man, whereby it is declared what he is.

---

¹ I have not been able to consult this work of Daneau, which is very rare, and not mentioned in the Bodleian Catalogue.

"φύσις, *i.e.* Nature, adds to the mere essence the essential and natural properties, as in man these are the capacity for learning, capacity also for knowledge, immortality (in the soul), risibility, speech; for these we say are natural to man, and his natural properties."

"μορφή adds to the essence and to the essential and natural properties other accidentals, which follow the true nature of the thing, and by which, as it were by lineaments and colours, οὐσία and φύσις are fashioned and depicted, as in man to have the face turned up towards heaven, from which he is also called ἄνθρωπος, and as also the being endowed with such or such a form of body and limbs, etc."

On these definitions we may remark that οὐσία, φύσις, and μορφή are properly metaphysical terms, not logical; and Zanchi's attempt to find equivalents for them in terms of the Aristotelian Logic involves much error and confusion.

In Aristotle, says Bishop Lightfoot,[1] "the form" (which is the aggregate of the qualities) "he calls indifferently εἶδος or μορφή. He moreover designates it by various synonyms. It is sometimes 'the abstract conception realised' (τὸ τί ἦν εἶναι), sometimes 'the essence corresponding to the definition' (ἡ οὐσία ἡ κατὰ τὸν λόγον), sometimes 'the definition of the essence' (ὁ λόγος τῆς οὐσίας), sometimes 'the definition' alone, sometimes 'the essence' alone."

Every one of these designations shows that οὐσία, as defined by Zanchi, and identified with τὸ τί ἦν εἶναι, is included in the 'form' (μορφή) and inseparable from it.

[1] *Philippians*, p. 126.

φύσις is not a logical term, and its definition by Zanchi, as "adding to the mere essence the essential and natural properties," is entirely arbitrary, and inconsistent with the use of the word by Aristotle.

In *Metaph.* iv. 1. 3, he classes φύσις as a first principle (ἀρχή) with thought and will and essence, and the final cause; and in iv. 4, 8 he says that "nature properly so called is the essence of things which have their efficient cause in themselves, by reason of what they are."[1]

Dr. Bruce unfortunately did not carry on his quotation from Zanchi beyond the three paragraphs quoted on p. 122 f., and so fell into the mistake of supposing, not very unnaturally, that Zanchi meant to *limit* the meaning of μορφή to those "other accidentals" which, he says, it "adds to the essence and to the

[1] Cf. Sir A. Grant, *Eth. Nic.* ii. 1. 2, n. 3.

essential and natural properties." Accordingly, Dr. Bruce makes the following comment: "Thus understood, μορφή presupposes οὐσία and φύσις, and yet is separable from them; it cannot exist without them, but they can exist without it. The Son of God, subsisting in the form of God, must have possessed divine οὐσία and divine φύσις: but it is conceivable that, retaining the οὐσία and the φύσις, He might part with the μορφή. And in point of fact such a parting for a season with the μορφή seems clearly taught in this place. The Apostle conceives of the Incarnation as an exchange of the divine form for the human form of existence."

Dr. Bruce is so eminently fair and candid, both in his quotations and in the inferences which he draws from them, that I feel sure he would not have put this interpretation upon Zanchi's definitions, if he had observed the paragraphs which follow immediately after the passage already quoted.

I must indeed plead guilty to having myself fallen into the same error with Dr. Bruce, through fixing my attention rather upon his comments on the abbreviated quotation than upon Zanchi's own application of his definitions to the language of St. Paul, which is as follows:

"Accordingly μορφή embraces in itself both φύσιν and οὐσίαν: and is nothing else than οὐσία itself invested with all its properties.

"Thus in God, although whatever is God and in God is in reality His perfectly simple essence, yet in a certain manner the οὐσία is distinguished from the φύσις, that is, from His natural and essential properties, which are omnipotence, omniscience, goodness, etc.

"However, the name μορφή, as we have said, embraces them all, with the further addition of glory and majesty to the Divine nature, and the figure of a true body to the human nature. LET THIS BE OUR CONCLUSION: by this phrase the Apostle has expressed the most perfect Divine nature in Christ, which he presently calls τὸ εἶναι ἴσα (*id est ἴσως*) Θεῷ, just as he presently expresses the whole and perfect human nature by the term μορφὴ δούλου."

If it is difficult to reconcile this with the author's previous definition of μορφή, we can forgive the inconsistency for the sake of the true conclusion. Only here also Zanchi falls into another error in identifying μορφὴ Θεοῦ with τὸ εἶναι ἴσα Θεῷ.[1]

When we pass on to modern theologians, we find that the errors of the first Protestant

[1] *see* p. 49 f.

Reformers in Germany have exercised an unfortunate influence on the interpretation of the passage even to the present day among writers who by no means admire the general theology of either Luther or Calvin.

The Doctrine of the Incarnation is the title of a learned and important work by the Rev. R. L. Ottley, Canon Gore's successor as Principal of the Pusey House, Oxford, and Bampton Lecturer for the present year, 1897.

The book has been subjected to a close and searching criticism in the *Church Quarterly Review* for October 1896, where the Reviewer draws attention to much that is "admirable," and says very justly that "the whole work is marked by reverence and high tone."

It is from no want of reverence that Mr.

Ottley, like so many before him, has failed to give a clear and consistent interpretation of the great passage on which the true doctrine of the Incarnation so largely depends.

In Mr. Ottley's various definitions of the all-important word μορφή there is the same vagueness and inconsistency which we have observed in Canon Gore's remarks on the same word.[1]

"This phrase," Mr. Ottley says, "implies possession of all the characteristic and essential attributes of Deity: μορφή is not to be confounded with οὐσία, but only one who was God could subsist ἐν μορφῇ Θεοῦ."[2]

The statement, though not actually incorrect, leaves too much room for misunderstanding: μορφή not only "implies," but necessarily includes in itself, both "οὐσία" and "all the characteristic and essential

[1] See p. 80 f.   [2] *Ottley*, i. 103.

attributes of Deity," as has been shown above on pp. 26 ff., 127 f.

In the note (3) on this statement, Mr. Ottley says, in reference to Chrysostom's identification of μορφή and φύσις — "It would be more strict to say, perhaps, that the Son of God could part with μορφὴ Θεοῦ, but not with οὐσία or φύσις Θεοῦ."

Among the writers to whom in particular Mr. Ottley feels himself under obligation we find the name of Dr. Bruce: and it is evident that we are here listening to an echo of Dr. Bruce's statement which we have noticed above: "The Son of God, subsisting in the form of God, must have possessed divine οὐσία and divine φύσις: but it is conceivable that, retaining the οὐσία and the φύσις, He might part with the μορφή."

We have shown above (p. 125 f.) how Dr. Bruce was misled by an ambiguous phrase in Zanchi's definition of μορφή: and here we see that Mr. Ottley has fallen into the same confusion, when, after writing that ὑπάρχων ἐν μορφῇ Θεοῦ "implies possession of all the characteristic and essential attributes of Deity," and again "the form of a servant (μορφὴν δούλου), *i.e.* the essential attributes of a servant," he contradicts himself by saying that "the Son of God could part with μορφὴ Θεοῦ, but not with οὐσία or φύσις Θεοῦ."

Again, when Mr. Ottley says that "The word μορφή in fact comprises all *those qualities which convince us of the real presence of a being or object*," he seems to be really describing not μορφή but σχῆμα,[1] and expressing in other words Zanchi's ambiguous definition of μορφή, namely, that it adds to the essential and natural properties other

[1] See Meyer's good definition of σχῆμα on p. 51.

accidentals which follow the nature of the thing, and *by which, as it were by lineaments and colours,* οὐσία and φύσις *are fashioned and depicted.*[1] This is, in fact, what is expressed in our passage by τὸ εἶναι ἴσα Θεῷ.

After differing so widely from Mr. Ottley as to the meaning of the important word μορφή, it is a pleasure to be able to defend him against an objection brought by his critic in the *Church Quarterly Review* on another point. "Mr. Ottley," it is said, "fails to show reason for his view that τὸ εἶναι ἴσα Θεῷ means the 'equality in state' with its 'glory and bliss,' as distinct from the common possession of the Divine attributes, or for his assumption that our Lord in the Incarnation parted with this τὸ εἶναι ἴσα Θεῷ."

I believe that Mr. Ottley's views are right

[1] The italics in both passages are mine.

on both points, and in support of them I may refer to what I have written above (pp. 38 f.) on the meaning of the phrase ἴσα Θεῷ and its relation to μορφὴ Θεοῦ: and if Mr. Ottley has given no reasons "for his assumption that our Lord in the Incarnation parted with this τὸ εἶναι ἴσα Θεῷ," he may possibly have supposed that it must be as clear to others as to himself that the logical connexion of the antithetical clauses necessarily excludes every interpretation, except that of the Synod of Antioch, κενώσας ἑαυτὸν ἀπὸ τοῦ εἶναι ἴσα Θεῷ.[1]

If Mr. Ottley's interpretation of the passage had been as correct generally as it seems to be on these points, it would probably have saved him from attempting to draw from St. Paul's language some inferences which it by no means warrants.

[1] See above, p. 73.

Dr. Otto Pfleiderer, Professor of Theology at Berlin, is well known in England by his *Hibbert Lectures* 1885, and his earlier and more important work *Paulinism*, published by the Committee of the "Theological Translation Fund."

His interpretation of "*the form of God*" is not based on any careful investigation of the meaning of μορφή, but on a pre-conceived idea of Christ as the pre-existent "heavenly man."

Referring to 1 Cor. xv. 47: *The second man is from heaven*, he argues that "this human person who had his origin *from* heaven, had also pre-existed *in* heaven *as man*, that is to say, as '*spiritual man*,' as the *same subject*, and in the *same form of existence*, as that in which he continues to live again in heaven as the exalted one."[1]

[1] *Paulinism*, i. 138 f.

In reference to 2 Cor. iv. 4, 6, where St. Paul speaks of the exalted Christ as "*the image of God*," and of "*the glory of God in the face of Jesus Christ*," Dr. Pfleiderer writes, "it is perfectly intelligible that the pre-existent Christ also, with reference to this form of appearance in the image of God, is described as ἐν μορφῇ Θεοῦ ὑπάρχων. This by no means implies that he himself was also God (Θεὸς ὁ λόγος); on the contrary, the Pauline notion of being in the image of God, as we have already seen, distinctly includes within itself that of being the pattern of humanity."

In the note on this passage he refers to Phil. iii. 20 f., "Christ will change our body of humiliation into one made like to the body of his glory." "What else, he asks, can we understand by this σῶμα τῆς δόξης αὐτοῦ than that very μορφὴ Θεοῦ in which the exalted one as well as the pre-existent was clothed? But in that case this μορφὴ Θεοῦ also contains nothing which lies outside of the notion of the εἰκὼν τοῦ υἱοῦ [Θεοῦ], Rom. viii. 29, or that of the δεύτερος ἄνθρωπος ἐξ οὐρανοῦ, whose image we shall all one day bear (1 Cor. xv. 47-49)."

Again Dr. Pfleiderer writes,[1] "The expression πᾶν τὸ πλήρωμα (1 Col. i. 19) is, according to the parallel passage (ii. 9), the fulness of the Godhead, the concentration of all the powers which constitute the Divine nature. Paul never says that these dwell in Christ, not even in Phil. ii. 6, where the μορφὴ Θεοῦ refers only to the form of His appearance, the σῶμα τῆς δόξης (see above): but that this fulness of the Godhead should have taken up its abode in the *earthly* Christ (for so we must understand Col. i. 19, on

[1] *Paulinism*, i. 146.

account of its connexion with ver. 20) is directly contradictory to that which we shall shortly see to have been the older Pauline view of Christ's becoming man."

By thus misinterpreting μορφὴ Θεοῦ as meaning only "the form of appearance" and so opposing it to "the fulness of the Godhead," Pfleiderer comes to the portentous conclusion that "if we are unwilling to pronounce the Epistle to the Colossians altogether spurious, there appears to be scarcely any other way out of the difficulty than to suppose that this, as well as other passages of this Epistle, was tampered with at a later period."

In answer to such speculations it is sufficient to refer to our previous investigation of the true meaning of μορφὴ Θεοῦ (pp. 22-36).

Again, after quoting Phil. ii. 5-8, Dr. Pfleiderer writes:[1] "It has been already remarked on the words ἐν μορφῇ Θεοῦ ὑπάρχων, that they mean nothing else than the εἰκών and δόξα Θεοῦ.

"The only difficulty is in the words οὐχ ἁρπαγμὸν ἡγήσατο τὸ εἶναι ἴσα Θεῷ. . . . They are opposed to ἐκένωσεν ἑαυτόν, that is to the self-sacrificing mode of action of which Christ is held up as an example. . . . They express in a figurative manner the disposition and mode of action of one who in selfish arrogance only τὰ ἑαυτοῦ σκοπεῖ."

So far we could hardly wish for a better explanation of the clause: but from this point Pfleiderer begins to fall into the errors which have been discussed above (p. 52 f.), of making τὸ εἶναι ἴσα Θεῷ, something higher than μορφὴ Θεοῦ, something to be

[1] *Paulinism*, i. 147.

obtained by renouncing this latter, instead of that which was itself renounced. He makes his meaning, however erroneous, too clear to be mistaken: "What Christ might have striven after in this selfish, grasping manner, if he had wished it, is expressed by the words τὸ εἶναι ἴσα Θεῷ. They must therefore indicate something beyond and above that which he already had, the μορφὴ Θεοῦ: and this can only be the dignity of supreme Lordship and equality with God, the absolute, perfect, sovereign Majesty, which belongs to God alone and to no other, not even to the Son who was the very image of Him as regards the form in which he appeared.

"He emptied himself (instead of coveting that which was greater and higher) of that which he justly possessed (namely of the μορφὴ Θεοῦ).

"Paul, after what he has said elsewhere,

can hardly have ascribed to Christ an actual εἶναι ἴσα Θεῷ." [1]

In the *Hibbert Lectures* (p. 58) we are told that "God has sent his Son into terrestrial life, in a body of flesh similar to our own, and by means of birth from a woman.

"As Paul understood it, this was not an 'incarnation' (*Menschwerdung*) in the strict doctrinal sense, inasmuch as the Son of God was really the celestial man and head of the human race before his appearance on the earth; he did not need, therefore, to take upon him a human nature, as orthodox theology teaches, but, according to Paul, he simply exchanged the form of his celestial existence, or his godlike body of light for the earthly form of existence, or a body of flesh like that of men."

[1] p. 148, note 1.

This "we may express in modern forms of thought by saying, *he is the embodied Ideal of religious and divine humanity, of its filial relationship to God, and of fraternal love between its own members.*"

It is needless to say that in fantastic speculations of this kind we can discover no resemblance to the real meaning of the passage. But I have given Pfleiderer's views at large in his own words, because they express very clearly a notion which pervades a great part of German theology, and is upheld, as we have seen (p. 120), by so important a writer as Dr. Dorner, I mean the representation of Christ as the Ideal Man pre-existing in the thought of God.

Hilgenfeld expresses the same view with equal plainness : "The Pauline Christ is indeed *the heavenly man*, but no divine being;"[1] and again, "The ἐν μορφῇ Θεοῦ ὑπάρχειν, which is attributed to Christ before his appearance as man, is explained, without reference to Philo's Logos-doctrine, from the conception of the heavenly Christ, attached even to Dan. vii. 13. The equality with God (*Gottgleichheit*), however, is first won through Christ's self-humiliation, and consists in the name which is above every name, in which all knees in heaven, on earth, and under the earth do bow."[2]

No theological work, we are told, has caused more excitement, or had a wider influence in Germany, during the last twenty years than Dr. Albrecht Ritschl's *Christian Doctrine of Justification and Reconciliation.*

It has been subjected to a severe but not unmerited criticism by L. Stählin in a volume

[1] *Zeitschrift*, 1871, p. 197.
[2] *Einleitung in d. N. T.*, p. 339.

entitled *Kant, Lotze, and Ritschl,* of which an English translation has been published by Messrs. T. and T. Clark of Edinburgh.

"*An Exposition and Critique of the Theology of A. Ritschl*" is the work of an ardent admirer, Julius Thikotter, which has been translated into French by another enthusiastic disciple, M. Aquiléra, a Protestant pastor, under the ambitious title, *The Theology of the Future.*

To avoid the possibility of misrepresentation, I shall quote from the admirer rather than from the critic, as I have only the first and not the second edition of Ritschl's own work at hand.

In dealing with such a subject, it was, of course, impossible for the author to avoid declaring what he thought of Christ Himself: and though Ritschl, as far as I have observed, gives no express interpretation of our passage, we are left in no doubt as to the meaning which he attached to the all-important clause ἐν μορφῇ Θεοῦ ὑπάρχων.

"Ritschl acknowledges a pre-existence of Christ, but this pre-existence is ideal, it is founded on the immutable will and eternal love of God, who determined before the foundation of the world that the unique Son should be the head of the Church which He was in some manner to embrace."[1]

Ritschl's professed object is to release the Christian religion from all metaphysical accretions. But what can be more entirely metaphysical than this notion of an ideal pre-existence of Christ in the thought of God?

Again we are told that, according to Ritschl, "The term *divinity* applied to Jesus expresses, in fact (*au fond*), nothing else

[1] *Théologie de l'Avenir*, p. 57.

than the absolute confidence of the believer in the redemptive power of the Saviour (Ritschl, iii. p. 360-368)."[1]

May we not then acknowledge a divine revelation in Christ's own statements concerning His relation to the Father, and in the statements of his Apostles concerning Him?

"We must not seek in the New Testament a *doctrine* on the divinity of Jesus Christ, but simply the expression of the religious experiences of the first believers in their contact with his person. The classical passages, such as Philippians ii. 6-11, Colossians i. 14-20, 2 Corinthians iv. 11, contain, in fact, nothing else than these experiences, the unique importance of the person of the Christ for the community which he founds, and in a secondary way for the universe in general.

[1] *Théologie de l'Avenir*, p. 116.

The same point of view dominates the Prologue of John (iii. p. 370, 376)."[1]

Thus in interpreting the language of St. Paul we are forbidden to connect it with a Divine revelation contained in Christ's declarations of His relation to the Father, or granted to St. Paul himself, as he frequently asserted.

From the author of such a theory we cannot expect help in determining what St. Paul himself meant by such a description as ὑπάρχων ἐν μορφῇ Θεοῦ.

Dr. Harnack's explanation of the passage demands attention rather from the high reputation of the author than for any light that it throws upon the real meaning of the Apostle.

In common with many others he regards the doctrine of the Divine pre-existence as a

[1] *Théologie de l'Avenir*, p. 117.

mere reflexion in St. Paul's mind of the glorified humanity in which he had first beheld the risen Christ.[1]

"According to one of the Apostle's ways of regarding the matter, Christ, after the accomplishment of his work, became the πνεῦμα ζωοποιοῦν through the resurrection.

"But the belief that Jesus always stood before God as the heavenly man, suggested to Paul the other view, that Christ was always a 'spirit,' that He was sent down by God, that the flesh is consequently something inadequate, and indeed hostile to Him, that He nevertheless assumed it in order to extirpate the sin dwelling in the flesh, that He therefore humbled Himself by appearing, and that this humiliation was the deed He performed.

[1] Harnack, *History of Dogma* (Theological Translation Library), vol. i. p. 327.

"This view is found in 2 Cor. viii. 9 (Ἰησοῦς Χριστὸς) δι' ὑμᾶς ἐπτώχευσεν πλούσιος ὤν, in Rom. viii. 3 ὁ Θεὸς τὸν ἑαυτοῦ υἱὸν πέμψας ἐν ὁμοιώματι σαρκὸς ἁμαρτίας καὶ περὶ ἁμαρτίας κατέκρινε τὴν ἁμαρτίαν ἐν τῇ σαρκί, and in Phil. ii. 5f. ὃς ἐν μορφῇ Θεοῦ ὑπάρχων . . . ἐταπείνωσεν ἑαυτόν, κ.τ.λ.

"In both forms of thought Paul presupposes a real exaltation of Christ.

"Christ receives after the resurrection more than he ever possessed (τὸ ὄνομα τὸ ὑπὲρ πᾶν ὄνομα). In this view Paul retains a historical interpretation of Christ, even in the conception of the πνεῦμα Χριστός.

"But whilst many passages seem to imply that the work of Christ began with suffering and death, Paul shows in the verses cited that he already conceives the appearance of Christ on earth as his moral act, as a humiliation, purposely brought about by God and Christ Himself, which realises its culminating point in the death on the cross.

"Christ, the divine spiritual being, is sent by the Father from heaven to earth, and of his own free will He obediently takes this mission upon Himself. He appears in the ὁμοίωμα σαρκὸς ἁμαρτίας, dies the death of the cross, and then, raised by the Father, ascends again into heaven, in order henceforth to act as the Κύριος ζώντων and (*sic*) νεκρῶν, and to become to His own people the principle of a new life in the spirit."

In an interesting and important work on *The Principle of the Incarnation*, the Rev. H. C. Powell has recently discussed from a psychological point of view the nature and limits of human knowledge, and the essential difference between it and the Divine manner of knowing, and has applied his conclusion thus formed to the relation between our Lord's divine and human knowledge.

In Book II. he deals with the Incarnation from a theological point of view, with especial reference to the Kenotic theory; and Book III. is devoted to a careful examination of the evidence of the Gospels concerning our Lord's knowledge during His life on earth.

The only part of the work with which we are especially concerned is the interpretation of Phil. ii. 5-7 in Book II. pp. 237-255.

Of the points which Mr. Powell selects as "of especial exegetical importance" the following seem most important:—

(1) The emphatic position of ἑαυτόν before ἐκένωσεν does not "convey that it was Himself, after the analogy of a vessel, that our Lord emptied, and so lend countenance to the idea that He actually

laid aside something *internal* to Himself."
St. Paul's intention was to bring out the
thoroughly *voluntary* character of our Lord's
self-humiliation. "Interpreters ancient and
modern are entirely agreed upon this point.
No one, as far as the present writer is
aware, has, *on exegetical grounds*, taken the
other view."

(2) All that can be got out of "the words
ἑαυτὸν ἐκένωσεν, *emptied Himself*, is that
our Lord did, in some manner not precisely
specified, voluntarily divest or empty Himself of something either internal to or
external to Himself. We must look beyond
these two words to determine *what* it was
which our Lord divested Himself of, and
in what manner, etc."

(3) and (4) In answer to the question,
Why did St. Paul not insert a defining
genitive after ἐκένωσεν? Mr. Powell replies

that "the participial clauses which follow do not exactly take the place of a defining genitive, but by explaining the manner in which our Lord emptied Himself they virtually indicate what it was which He emptied Himself of." ... "Because of the three possible alternatives—external glories, internal attributes, or both—the emptying or divesting Himself of the external glories of Deity would be a natural and direct consequence of taking the servant's form. By the very act of doing this, our Lord concealed His Godhead. But no emptying of the internal attributes or essence of the Godhead would be a similar consequence."

. The direct and complete answer to the question, *What* did our Lord resign? is that which Bishop Ellicott appears to have indicated in a letter to Mr. Powell: "Would not the logically exact genitive be τοῦ εἶναι ἴσα Θεῷ? This 'aequal*iter* esse' He gave up, and in the manner specified in the participial clauses."

Bishop Ellicott thus agrees with Bishops Westcott and Lightfoot, and with the Synod of Antioch. See above pp. 48, 55, 73. Such a consensus should be decisive for English scholars.

M. Godet, the learned Professor of Theology in the Reformed Church at Neuchatel, whose Commentaries and other works are so well known in England, and in many respects so admirable, has been led into some very vague and inconsistent statements through his erroneous interpretation of St. Paul's language in Philippians.

Thus in his *Defence of the Christian Faith*, p. 288, he writes: "Before He appeared here below, He existed '*in the form of God*,' that is to say, in a state of

Deity; it was by His own will that He became man, after He had 'emptied Himself,' to take upon Him the form of a servant."

Again on p. 297: "The Divine manner of being, I must acknowledge, is not compatible with our present human manner of existence. But that is precisely the reason on account of which Scripture teaches two things: first, that Jesus had to lay down His divine manner of existence — His 'form of God'—in order to become man; second, that in order to regain His divine condition, a glorious transformation was effected in His humanity by means of the Ascension. I say, a laying down, a stripping of Himself. St. Paul describes this supreme event in these words, 'He who was in the form of God emptied Himself, and took upon Him the form of a servant.'"

By leaving out the intermediate clause, "counted it not a prize that He was on an equality with God," Godet makes it appear that Christ emptied Himself of the "form of God."

In like manner he says again, "In Philippians . . . he speaks of Christ as having by nature '*the form of God*,' the divine manner of being, and then, at the moment of His appearing here below, renouncing this equality with God to which He had a right, taking upon Him voluntarily '*the form of a servant*,' —that is the human condition, etc."[1]

Elsewhere[2] he writes: "The idea of this divestiture of the divine state and of the entrance into the conditions of the human state is expressed by St. Paul still more clearly in another statement, Phil. ii. 6-8: "Who, although He was in form of God, did

---
[1] *Defence*, p. 322.
[2] *Études Bibliques*, p. 134.

not avail Himself of it to appear as a God; but stripped Himself in taking the form of a servant, and appeared in the likeness of men, being found in all things such as a man."

It is in this vague and inadequate conception of μορφὴ Θεοῦ as identical with τὸ εἶναι ἴσα Θεῷ, and therefore meaning a "divine state," "a divine manner of being," that M. Godet's erroneous inferences have their root. He makes the κένωσις consist in laying aside not only the metaphysical attributes of God, as omnipotence, omniscience omnipresence, but also the moral attributes of immutable holiness, and perfect infinite love, and, most surprising of all, His personal consciousness: "He knew Himself as Son, with that knowledge with which the Father Himself knew Him eternally, and—here is the self-stripping (*dépouillement*) on which all the foregoing depend — *that consciousness of Sonship, which was His light, He let it be extinguished within Him,* to retain only His inalienable personality, His 'ego' endowed with liberty and intelligence as every human 'ego'; for our personality is formed in the image of His. In virtue of this abasement He was able to enter into a human development completely similar to ours."[1]

That so devout a believer as M. Godet could entertain such a thought as is expressed in the words which I have emphasised by italics, is a remarkable instance of the extreme danger of metaphysical speculation on so profound a mystery as the Incarnation,— a danger immensely increased when speculation is founded upon false inferences from an erroneous interpretation of the language of Holy Scripture.

[1] *Études Bibl.* p. 135.

In justice, however, to M. Godet we must remember that however erroneous the Kenotic views into which he was thus led by his misunderstanding of St. Paul's language, he never consciously adopted any theory of Christ's Person inconsistent with His pre-existence as the very and eternal Son of God. Of that primary truth Dr. Godet was always a most earnest and devout advocate, as we may learn from the following and many other passages of the works which we have been quoing :—

"Every time that I consider this question before God, three convictions seize me, laying hold at the same time of my mind and heart.

"First, that it is impossible to detract anything from the doctrine of the essential and personal divinity of the Christ, without at the same time infringing equally upon the belief in the intimacy of the relation between God and man.

"Secondly, that whatever detracts from the essential and personal divinity of our Lord, detracts equally from the horror which we feel at that which separates us from God, that is sin.

"Thirdly, that whatever we detract from the essential and personal divinity of our Lord, detracts *ipso facto* equally from the glorious reality of Christian holiness."[1]

I have quoted these words of M. Godet not only in justice to him, but also because I believe that they represent the most cherished convictions of others, whose interpretation of Philippians ii. 5-11 I have had occasion to criticise.

If some of the ablest and most influential

[1] *Defence*, p. 325.

theologians of our own Church have drawn, as we believe, erroneous and dangerous inferences from a mistaken exegesis of St. Paul's language, we must not forget that in other branches of theology they have proved themselves to be most earnest, devout, and enlightened advocates of the chief doctrines of the Christian Faith.

If anything that I have written should give pain to such men, let me end this little volume by a humble apology for this and its many other faults, and let me try to make my peace with all who love truth for truth's sake in the oft-quoted words of Aristotle: ἄμφοιν γὰρ ὄντοιν φίλοιν ὅσιον προτιμᾶν τὴν ἀλήθειαν.

www.ingramcontent.com/pod-product-compliance
Lightning Source LLC
Chambersburg PA
CBHW022117160426
43197CB00009B/1059